Copyright © 2024 Krystal Kaye Portorreal

All rights reserved. No part of this publication may be reproduced, distributed, or transmitted in any form or by any means, including photocopying, recording, or other electronic or mechanical methods, without the prior written permission of the publisher, except in the case of brief quotations embodied in critical reviews and certain other noncommercial uses permitted by copyright law.

ISBN: 9798884762039

CONTENTS

Dedication		7
Introduction		9
Lesson 1	CLASS IN SESSION	11
Lesson 2	SURVIVAL	21
Lesson 3	HOW DID I GET HERE?	49
Lesson 4	STRIPPER POLE TO THE FLAG POLE	65
Lesson 5	MILITARY TIES	81
Lesson 6	SENT TO SAVE	95
Lesson 7	DOORS TO DIVORCE	109
Lesson 8	A SAMPLE OF SUCCESS	117
Lesson 9	ROCK BOTTOM	123
Lesson 10	FINDING FAITH	135
Lesson 11	GETTING DOWN TO BUSINESS	141
About the Author		151

DEDICATION

To the man who has loved me through it all. My best friend, my lover, my partner. The man that showed me what being loved by a man truly feels like. I love you forever, my husband, Lavob Portorreal.

To the light of my eye, the beat of my heart, the woman that has always prayed for me and believed in me more than I could ever believe in myself. My momma, Debbie Ann Roberson.

INTRODUCTION

There are moments in our lives that leave impressions so deep that they become part of our makeup. A part of who we are forever. These moments are what I like to refer to as lessons.

Lessons can come in many forms, some good, some bad, but we learn something from them either way.

Moving into purpose takes so much courage because to do so, you must first address the lessons you've learned your entire life. You must stare into the face of the lessons that made you happy, but also the lessons that broke you.

I believe that confidence is the starting place of purpose. A synonym for confidence is courage. We must all be courageous as we walk into the purpose that God has for our lives. He has called every one of us to something very specific, and to uncover that, we must constantly listen to him, taking action on the courageous things he is asking us to do.

I wasn't always this confident. I spent the better part

of my life broken on the inside, which manifested in all sorts of unimaginable ways.

In the pagers that follow, I will describe some of the ways the lessons broke me, but you will also see how those lessons were all a part of God's plan.

Even though I had turned my back on God, he never left my side, and his plans never changed. My hope is that as you read the following story full of heartbreak and breakthrough, you will start to understand your own purpose. My hope is that you will have moments with God as you read and start to understand just how much the world needs your brilliance.

Lesson 1

CLASS IN SESSION

My childhood was full of lessons, ones that would haunt me and some that would set me free later in life. To guide you to the starting place of purpose, I must first take you to the time and place where I began to learn these life lessons.

Discovering Daddy

It's natural that I begin with my father because so many of my memories are directly tied to him, and I ended up being more like him than I ever knew I would. Sometimes those that hurt us the most make the deepest impression.

My dad stood about 6'7, and maybe a buck 80. He was a playful person, always telling jokes or making up silly rhymes, and he called me his baby girl. He was the first man I ever really loved. He was also the first man that made me feel like I was unworthy of love.

My very first memory of him is a happy one. We lived in Ada, Oklahoma, and I was about five years old. We were riding in the car, and he was just being his goofy self and making up rhymes for us. "Get in the car, you bubble-headed jar"…just the absolute silliness that was my dad. At that time, I didn't realize my dad had some serious demons that would literally plague my childhood. Often, parents don't realize that when they refuse to heal, the blood from their wounds drips all over the children and their children's, children. The refusal to get help is literally the beginning of generational curses.

I started to realize my daddy was different not long after that car ride when my mother made him sleep outside on the porch one night after he came home. He came home drunk, and she was not having it, so he slept outside. It was also around this time that I realized the smell my father always had, the smell I had come to remember about him the most, wasn't cologne, it was alcohol. I literally thought my daddy just always smelled good.

I'm not sure how or at what point I realized the smell was alcohol, but it began to tear away at my soul every time. It became something that was tied to so much pain in my life. I can't believe I ever picked it up myself and took a drink. But more on that later.

My dad's addictions continued for years, and alcohol slowly progressed into full-out drug use. Later on, he got addicted to crack cocaine. My comedian dad, who sang goofy, made-up songs with us in the car, spent part of his life addicted to crack. It sounds absolutely insane saying it out loud. **But *there is a very valuable lesson here for ALL of us:* When we let the enemy in, he knows no bounds.** For the devil, alcohol addiction is just a short distance away from drug abuse. Because it's that same spirit. Right now, you may be struggling with alcohol addiction and telling yourself that you would NEVER do any drugs. Well, I'm here to tell you that if you have allowed yourself to become ok with any addiction, you are just a short walk away from another one.

Addiction is insidious and very slow acting. It literally sneaks up on you in the most devilish way. One moment you are having fun in the bars with your friends as a 20-year-old, and the next thing you know, you are throwing up blood and still drinking at 35. Then you're having your first drink at 11 am if you have a meeting coming up...just to take the edge off. I will touch more on my own addictions later, but I want you to catch this lesson because it may save your life. Don't give that spirit an open door in your life because addiction is one of the biggest blessing blockers!

It will take over and strip you of ambition and self-confidence before you even notice. You CANNOT get a breakthrough if you are allowing addiction to plague your life. If you are letting that spirit sit on your chest, you cannot get up and do the things that God has called you to do. So release it. We will dive more into this later. For now, I want to continue to the next person who had a significant effect on me. My momma.

The Teachings of Momma

They say the ones that are doing well often go unnoticed. Well, for a long time, my mom was that person. She was a constant in my life. She always appeared happy, always singing and praying for us. She was literally my rock, even though it was a while before I recognized it. She is now my best friend, and I will always believe her prayers brought me back after all I am about to describe to you.

At the time, while I was figuring out that my dad had serious demons he was fighting, my mom was the shining light in my life! I can confidently say she is the only reason I'm here today. She is responsible for the happiest memories of my life, and I will always thank her for that. Now, looking back, I have no idea how she kept it all together.

Sometimes happiness, even if genuine, can teach some very valuable lessons. And there are some very important lessons I learned from my mom's happiness that I want to share with you. These are lessons that you, too, may have learned from your mother. All of us are more connected through generational ties than we realize. Some of the lesson's momma taught me are ones that have been passed down from my ancestors. Happiness leaves clues, too, not just pain. We must learn from them and dig deeper to understand WHY someone is happy. I capitalized "why" because the word "why" will come into play when I teach you the *Confident Brand System* in the last chapter. *So, let's get into the lessons momma taught me:*

Teaching #1: God can always bring joy. No matter what chaos is going on around us, you can turn to him, and he will bring joy during any situation. My mom would be praising and singing God's name in true and pure joy, even as my dad was home hungover and wreaking alcohol. This truly taught me that when times are rough, turning to God will ALWAYS bring joy. I know we've all heard the phrase "Give it to God".

Well, my mother practices that with expert skill! My mom never once allowed my dad's sins and trauma to make her feel unjoyful. You can tell when someone is faking it, and she wasn't. She was the happiest person I knew, and her joy was infectious all my life. Ya'll my mom would come home after working all day at school (she was a school teacher), then work her second job at Walmart, standing up all night at a register…and she would still be smiling. She never complained about the imperfect and sometimes traumatic life we were living. Anyone that knows me now, you know I'm an extremely joyful person as well. I am that way because I've chosen to give it all to God, exactly the way my momma did.

This is not ignoring the bad things that happen, but it's learning to FULLY trust God and that he will take care of everything. This valuable lesson would stick with me, even when I was not close to God throughout different periods in my life.

Teaching #2: No matter how bad things get, it is the woman's responsibility to keep things "together" for the family. All lessons, no matter how noble they are, are not good ones for us to learn and hold onto. This lesson is one of that nature. This lesson looked like my mom always putting everyone, including my dad, above herself.

This looked like her opting for a career in teaching vs. music because music wasn't responsible for the family. This looked like her staying with my dad for years despite his addictions. And this looked like her choosing to allow her dreams to be put off time and time again because everyone else had to be taken care of first. Now, obviously, I admire my dear momma so much for all she did for us. And this second lesson wasn't something she chose. It was something she *learned*. It's something that was learned and deeply rooted for generations.

This lesson was a learned behavior. All the women in my family are strong, and that strength sometimes makes us believe it's a badge of honor to put everyone else first. And you know what, I see this lesson being learned by many black women in the US. Many of us have learned that we are supposed to put everyone and everything in our lives before us. We have been conditioned to believe it's selfish to put ourselves first. This limiting belief is a generational curse. When you put others before yourself…you teach the next generation of women that their desires don't matter. Well, I want to break that thought pattern for you right now.

Women deserve the things they want right now. We must get out of this mentality that we can only have what we want after being drained and nearly depleted. You do not have to give everything first, THEN have what you desire.

Are you starting to see a clear picture of how the wounds of our parents have a massive effect on our lives? Are you starting to understand how generational curses and thought patterns are born and passed on? How are you shaping the thought patterns of generations of women in your family? Are you doing your part to break the generational curses in your bloodline? If not, allow me to help you with this word:

> *You do not have to be the oldest, the college graduate, or the parent, in your family to break generational curses. You can be the pioneer and help your family be released from the curses that bind! Stop waiting for someone else in your family to do it! Make a move!*

Be willing to break up with the cursed mentalities that have been plaguing you and your bloodline for years!

Teaching#3: Struggling financially is not an acceptable option. Now, I know I will lose some of you here because some mentalities still need to be shifted. But just hang on, and let this lesson help you with that. It was not uncommon for my mom to be working 2 or 3 jobs while raising us practically alone for most of our lives and still struggling! She would work so hard, and even with a professional degree, there was still a struggle. This is the story many of us have, right? We see momma working hard, with no father in the picture, and there never seems to be enough to get beyond just "getting by". Because of this, I knew that I wanted to get a job that would pay me a lot of money even at a young age. Early in life, I would say I wanted to be a doctor or a lawyer, and this was for one reason, to make enough money to support my family one day. And if I'm honest, I never remember just wanting to support my family. I've always wanted to be very wealthy. Because I didn't want to just get by.

    Just getting by looked like a constant battle and worry about where the next electric bill payment was going to come from! That was not acceptable to me. As Christian women, oftentimes, we pray for the bare minimum. We ask God *not* to bring us riches but to help us make enough to support our families. He answers those prayers every day as your light bill is paid, and food is put on the table. So, imagine if you asked for more? What reason do you have to believe he won't provide it? He hasn't let you down yet. Trust him and trust HIS process. You see, I've learned now that not asking God for exactly what we want is actually a sign of mistrust. We are so afraid that if we ask him for something too big for US to do alone, it won't happen. We are still relying on ourselves instead of fully trusting him. God will not release the blessing until you start trusting him enough to ask for exactly what you want!

What is something you have in your heart but have been too afraid to ask God for in your out-loud voice? Right now, I want you to ask him for that thing. No matter where you are, stop and ask him. Ask him boldly and expectantly. Then continue to ask him for that thing in that same way every day until it comes to fruition. And be ready to act when he brings the blessing.

I think many of us worry that we are demanding from God. We worry that we are not allowing God to control our lives if we ask for something specific. Well, I'm here to release you of that thought pattern right now. Because check this, God gave you the words. He gave you the thought and the vision. You didn't just dream up this thing that you want so badly! He gave you the vision and is just waiting for you to believe it and ask for it.

I will end this lesson with one last note. Being a Christian woman does not mean you can't be wealthy. You can have all the blessings of wealth that you desire. We are the daughters of a king and a father who cares about us deeply. He wants to fulfill our wildest dreams and even those greater than we could ever dream. God does not desire us to live in poverty and struggle. So, going forward in this book, I want you to release any mentality that a Christian woman cannot speak about wealth or have an abundance of it. Because chile…we are gonna talk about money! In fact, I have a whole chapter dedicated to telling you about my story with business success and how I made over $200k revenue in one year after never earning more than $3k in one month! So, buckle up and be ready to clutch your pearls if you are squeamish about the money conversation. But it will be had!

Lesson 2

SURVIVAL

The last chapter was the beginning. When you are just beginning, you are learning…you haven't developed the skills to survive just yet. So, at the beginning of the last chapter, I was still in complete innocence. I had no idea about my father's addiction, I was oblivious to some things going on, so I was just learning about this thing called life.

In this chapter, I explain how I used everything I learned, good and bad, and applied it to my life to survive. Now, survive is a powerful word for some people. For some, it means something very drastic and life-threatening. When I am talking about surviving in this chapter, it's in terms of some trauma and just me surviving the things that were happening in my life. You see, even though we associated survival with negative, you survive good things as well. Survival is learning how to cope! I remember reading once that both good and bad triggers can bring on stress in the body. Sometimes our body does not know the difference.

Literally, our fight or flight response behaves in the same way from good and bad stimuli. That is why it's so very important to learn how to respond to stimuli in the proper way, so your body is not going into overdrive every time you are happy or going through trauma!

Have you ever sat down and thought about your reactions to certain situations? Are you jumping into full fight or flight mode every time you get an email you don't like, or when a client decides not to work with you? Well, I challenge you to think about that while I break down this chapter. So, let's get to it.

The letter that broke me

Breakthrough requires studying the past. It requires a keen understanding of what happened to understand how we can move forward. My hope is for you to have a breakthrough. So, I must take you back to what broke me for you to understand and receive.

As I got older and the more I witnessed my dad's addiction, and the more I was told by my mom, the more I started to take my father's addictions personally. I could not understand why this man I loved so much would not stop drinking alcohol and using drugs. Why wouldn't he do it for me? I used to write my dad these letters asking him to please stop smoking and please stop drinking. I would leave them for him in different places around the house and watch how he reacted. Usually, he would fold the letter up and keep it. Or so I thought.

One time, my dad had stayed out drinking very late. I was old enough to know that when he didn't come home after work, he was out drinking, and those nights I would have the worst anxiety while lying in my bed. It was those nights that I would pray to God, not for my dad's salvation, but to thank him for my momma. I would thank him for giving me at least one stable parent who cared about me and cared for me no matter what.

But, back to the letter. I wrote him a very long letter this time, about two pages (it felt long, okay lol). I asked him to please give his life back to God and to stop drinking. I also poured out my heart and told him that his drinking hurt me and made me very sad and scared for him. I put the letter in a place I knew he would see it and waited for him to wake up.

We had a rental house that had a garage that had been converted into a basement of sorts. I remember him coming out of the basement where he basically lived by this point, smelling like his favorite cologne. I watched as he unfolded the letter and spent a few minutes reading it with a stone-cold face. This was confusing to me because when I wrote it, I was crying my eyes out. Then, in a move that literally broke my heart, he crumbled it up and threw it in the trash. I was devastated. At that moment, I felt like I was nothing to him. I didn't know anything deep about addiction at the time.

I just knew this man that I loved took something precious that I wrote to him and treated it like literal garbage. That was the moment I also began to crumble. I began to realize that no matter what I said or did, my dad's disease wasn't going away and I couldn't change that. In that moment and for many moments that followed, I felt just like that crumpled letter.

While I come from a family of criers, after that day, I was cold when it came to my dad. I still loved him, but he made a part of me shut down. It was like I knew that I had to protect myself. I knew that his life was spiraling, and I knew his demons wouldn't let him care about anything but alcohol and drugs, so I wouldn't allow myself to ever be hurt by him again. What I didn't know at the time is that the wall I was building with him was keeping me tied to the hurt. I built a fortress around my pain with myself inside. I imprisoned myself.

In the momma chapter, I told you that the good ones often go ignored. Well, during this time, while I was literally changing my whole personality because my dad hurt me, my momma was still there. She was still there, taking us to church, singing with us, and praying with us. And while I was singing and praying, I was also walling off parts of me to protect myself from my dad. This is where I learned the art of hiding things and having two faces in my life. This is the time in my life I can pinpoint learning to be secretive. Even though I didn't know it at the time, this was the start of my own addictive behavior. The secrecy is where it starts for me. I hid my feelings and walled them off in secret places …the exact behavior I displayed later when I was secretly hiding my alcohol abuse. You see, while I was going through all of this emotional trauma inside, I was the happiest person in the room. Not that the happiness wasn't genuine. But, I had taught myself to separate myself from the hurt when I needed to. It was the worst kind of lie. The one that you don't even know you are telling. This time in my life was pivotal for me on an emotional level. However, I was not the only one going through it! My mother was also just about at her breaking point.

Discern The Escalation: The Divorce

I can remember two distinct moments that I feel were the turning points for my mom regarding my dad's substance abuse. Moments when I KNEW she was tired and ready to leave and pretty much just waiting for the right moment. Moments when I know she was only one cast-iron skillet away from losing it on this man completely!

The first moment is one of the many times when my dad came home drunk and high one evening. I had gotten accustomed to lying in bed waiting for him to get back, even though I supposedly didn't care about him anymore. My baby brother and I shared a room with bunk beds, and my brother was on the bottom. As I lay there on the top bunk, wondering where he had been and waiting to hear him go into the basement like he always did on those nights, something different happened. My dad appeared in the doorway and turned on the light. As I'm pretending to wake up, my brother wakes up, and immediately my dad starts yelling at my brother to get up a be a man.

Now, my brother was maybe 5 or 6 at the time, so I'm not sure he knew exactly what was going on, but it was very scary. My dad was extremely drunk, and I knew that it wasn't him in that room with us; it was the alcoholic demon in his body. It seemed like forever, but somehow my mom and sister came into the room. My mom starts telling my dad he needs to go to bed and leave my brother alone. Now, momma had a way of being very calm while telling you that the wrath of God will come down if you don't stop.

The next thing I knew, my dad had escalated the yelling into pushing my brother's head down as my brother was trying to stand up. I just remember him yelling, "be a man", and pushing his head down hard. Finally, my mom said something (I don't remember what), that stopped him dead in his tracks, and he retreated to his pit we called the basement. After that night, I think we all felt a bit on edge. We saw that he was capable of being that violent drunk. This man was no small cookie! As I said, he was 6'7 and in fighting shape despite all of the alcohol and drugs! So, the thought of him being capable of violence was terrifying. This was a moment when I think my mom realized that she couldn't stay much longer. She knew that things were about to take a turn for the worst. She knew that as my brother grew, there would be another dynamic brought into this house that was on another level. For a long time, it had just been us girls, and my dad would never imagine hurting us. But, that night, we all saw that as the masculine energy grew in the home, things had the potential to go way left. This was the first turning point.

The next moment of escalation is a bit more dramatic. One evening, my dad was even more late than usual. I ended up falling asleep, and he didn't come home until the sun was up! Now, my brain is foggy on every detail (I think I've done that to protect myself), but I remember my mom somehow found out he was out all night, into the morning, with our next-door neighbor! My next-door neighbor was a sassy, single mother of three kids. She was one of those women that had no respect for the sanctity of marriage. I think my dad was drawn to her because he was able to feed his demons with her.

When my dad stayed out with this woman, we ALL saw another side of my mom! We saw a woman at her final breaking point! I don't remember everything that happened, but televisions were thrown, cuss words I had never heard were said, and the lady next door is actually lucky she didn't lose her life that day. And I'm not exaggerating at all.

The main thing that does stand out to me about this day is how we kids reacted to the trauma. As my mom yelling and throwing things all over the house for what felt like all day, all of us kids had different reactions happening. I was cheering her on, happy that she finally stood up to my dad, ready to leave.

Honestly, I think part of me was happy to have someone else feel toward him like I did. But while I was jumping up and down, my sister was cationic and stared out of her bedroom window for hours. I could tell she was deeply hurt by what was inevitably to come. We all knew there was no going back from this. It was over between momma and daddy, and I think my sister was facing that harsh reality in her own mind as she looked out of that window for hours. And finally, my baby brother. He seemed to be in and out of awareness of what was going on. He would have moments where he would be scared (maybe if he heard a bang), then he would be happy. Thinking about it now, it seems like he was going back and forth, mirroring how my sister and me were reacting. He was young and impressionable, and I think he just didn't really know how to feel.

This was the final breaking point. Shortly after that, my mom started driving around different neighborhoods with us, looking for rental houses after school or while my dad wasn't home or asleep in the basement.

One important lesson that sticks out to me during this period of my life is how my mother KNEW it was time to move because of the different situations being presented in our lives. **She was able to *discern the escalation* and make**

a quick decision from there to leave. Now, some will say she should've left way sooner, maybe so, but I truly believe there is divine timing for everything. I believe we all needed to see and experience the escalation. We needed this to be part of our story.

These lessons were lessons for us all. Each member of my family that experienced this time took something from it. And I truly believe we took something we needed. Something God needed us to have to fulfill our destiny. I now know that part of my destiny is telling my story.

This time in my life with my father ended just a few months after the overnight incident. My pastor at the time came to our home as we moved out our things and left my dad in basically an empty house with nothing but his pit of basement furniture. I guess the pastor was there to facilitate, but I remember him asking each of us to say how we were feeling at that moment. Everyone cried and said their piece. Everyone except me. I stone coldly said, "There is nothing left to say", even though my heart was literally BREAKING. At that moment, I felt extremely sorry for my dad. Even though I knew it was time to go, even though I was cheering my mom on. I was again feeling like that crumpled piece of paper, and my heart was in pieces.

That marked the final purging of any "daddy's baby girl" that was left in me. Although there would be more daddy confrontations and eventual healing, at that time, us moving out marked the end of our family as we knew it. I knew that this time, it was real. It wasn't a short separation like they had done in the past. There was an absoluteness in the air that no one could deny. As we pulled away from that house that day, I felt nothing but worry about my dad. I knew we were the only thing that was keeping his addiction somewhat in check. I knew that any trying he had done to get sober would go out of the window, and that demon would take him over. I was young, but I knew a spirit when I saw one, and I felt it strong when we left. I knew daddy would go off of the deep end.

Those feelings would turn into feelings of guilt later on when I found out he was in jail for strong-armed robbery. You see how unrealistic the mind of a child can sometimes be? I had no responsibility for us leaving him, but I somehow made myself feel bad that we left, and he ended up an extreme addict in jail. Again, everything happens for a reason because going to jail was probably the best thing that could've happened to him! He found salvation in jail and quit using drugs. In fact, when he got out of jail, he got remarried and started a whole new family. When my dad passed years later, his children from his other marriage missed a completely different man than me and my siblings did.

You see, I think many times people make the mistake of believing just because *they* got healed, the people they have hurt are healed as well. This is an untrue thing that addicts tell themselves. The pain you cause when you are an addict can haunt people for years, even after you are sober. The people you hurt along the way have their own journey to forgive you and release the pain you caused. Right now, there may be some of you reading this who know you have wronged someone in the past. However, you have gotten your life "right" and moved on. Listen…you cannot move on and just hope they find salvation for the pain you caused them. You need to make amends. It is unacceptable to get your blessing then just keep it moving. That's selfish and will block you from entering your blessings fully.

My promise to myself: Mirror talk

After we left my dad, we moved into some apartments and started school quickly. One thing that I remember about the beginning of this period in my life took place literally as soon as we moved into our new apartment.

After we moved everything in, the first thing I wanted to do was have a nice shower. So, I got into the shower, and while I was in there, I started to think about my dad again. I thought about what we had been through and where he would end up. When I emerged from the shower, I walked into my and my sister's bedroom. I'm not sure where she was, but she wasn't home because I remember being in our room completely naked and looking in our old school mirror attached to our white dresser. I stared at my naked body, and then I stared into my eyes. For some reason, as I stared into my own eyes, I saw my daddy.

I saw my dad staring back at me, and I felt an overwhelming sense of sadness all over my entire body. I broke down because I think it all hit me, that I was probably never going to see him again. Like I said before, I saw the demon on him when we left, and I knew he was gone…at the time, it felt like he would be gone forever.

So, as I began to gather myself from this spontaneous breakdown, I looked in the mirror once again and asked "daddy" (me), why wasn't I good enough for him to quit alcohol and drugs? I asked him why he didn't love me enough to quit. And the answers I told myself are actually hard to write. I told myself at that moment that I was ugly, that I was stupid, and that no one would ever love me. I was telling myself these things out loud.

What I didn't realize at that moment is that I opened a door for the enemy to walk right in. I gave him permission to come and plague me with low self-esteem and horrible relationships for years to come. It wasn't until YEARS later that I recanted that declaration because God laid it on my heart to do so. I know that's the reason I never forgot this one small moment of my life. I think God kept it top of mind because he knew one day I would need to take that back to survive.

So you see, regardless if we continue our close walk with God or not, he remembers us and takes care of us. He knows exactly where we will be in every moment of our lives, so he does little things to ensure we are on the right path. He leaves us clues.

Now, I can't talk about survival without talking about how I learned to survive. You see, we are students from the moment we are born into this world. We are constantly watching, listening, and learning how to behave. One of the important things we learn is how to survive. And we learn that from those around us.

Do As I Do

I spoke some in the last chapter about how my momma was always the breadwinner and constantly making sure we were good to go. Well, after we left daddy, that kicked into overdrive. I was too young to know exactly what was going on financially, but what I do know is momma was working her tail off. At one point, she was teaching all day, then working at Walmart on her feet until like 11 pm on weekdays and on weekends sometimes too! Thinking about it now, I have no clue how she was doing that. The hard work she put in during this time is just incredible. It's funny because I know that several of my black friends had moms doing the same thing.

It was not uncommon for a black woman to be working multiple jobs because she was a single parent. It's like we were all oblivious to the fact that this was not normal and not healthy. However, it's such a normal thing in the black community, so it didn't seem out of the ordinary.

I want to talk for a moment about desensitizing. What I'm talking about above is a prime example of this term. Because the situation of a black single mom working her tail off at 2 or 3 jobs, even if she has a college education, was SO common, we kids didn't think anything of it. Our community as a whole is really desensitized to trauma! Black women, in particular, are so used to certain things in our lives or in generations being common, that we forget that trauma is not normal and should not be tolerated.

Now, you gotta do what you gotta do, and that's exactly what momma did! I admire her for it and will thank her for the rest of my life. However, the deeper lessons are important to focus on here. These lessons are two-fold, both good and bad. In the previous chapter, I walked you through some teachings that momma gave. Now, I want to walk you through a few more lessons that I learned both from momma and just my environment as a whole as this point in my life. Things that would shape the person I would become.

The Lessons of Survival
Lesson #1: Never depend on a man

Now, this lesson may seem out of place because momma was by no means depending on my dad for anything when we were there. However, in order for her to be in the situation she was in at this time, there was some level of dependence *at some point*. At some point, she believed that my dad was the one, so she depended on him for love, affection, trust, security, and all of the things any of us want and need in a relationship. Then, at some point he just decided to stop providing those things. So, what I learned about survival was that I can never be hurt by a man if I never depend on a man. When people seek therapy, the therapist will often go back to your childhood first and foremost because we learn these things in a childlike state of mind and never re-learn them the right way as adults.

I can recognize now that trying to block myself off to never love a man is not at all healthy. It was one of the many lessons I had to unlearn as I grew older, and God showed me a better way. This lesson manifested itself by being super cold to the opposite sex for a very long time. Some would even say I was a b-word towards boys growing up! Because let me tell you, no boy, and I mean no boy, was getting past this gate to my heart with this lesson as the gatekeeper! So even as I moved through life and had relationships or "situations" with men, I never really let my guard down fully for a very long time. And when I did, things went a bit left. But we will talk about that soon. For now, let's move onto the next lesson.

Lesson #2: Higher Education is King

Now, I'm writing this lesson here because I think

many women in black families have a similar lesson. This one is a twofold lesson in that I learned something good and something "bad", and the bad part became a limiting belief I had to break later on.

Now, if there is one thing momma didn't play about was her education. She went back to school to get her bachelor's degree in education when we were young so that she could have a stable living for us. She became a teacher and never looked back. So, what's the lesson, you ask. I want to go back to the term "stable". In lower-class black families, often that is the standard. That is what we are reaching for, stability. If we can pay the bills, we are good to go, period. So, a lesson I learned here was that stability was above everything else.

Another part of this lesson, the part that makes it twofold, is that my mom originally never intended to be a teacher. She had a love for music and wanted to major in that. Why that didn't work out is her story to tell, but knowing she took a completely different path in life for stability taught me that stability was the number one important thing in a career. While getting a degree to have a stable job is not a bad thing, the idea that education is the only and BEST route to take presents some issues when you seek to be an entrepreneur later in life! It's hard to believe in yourself as an entrepreneur when all of your life you have learned that the only way to achieve stability is to have an education and a job working for someone else.

This is what people mean when they speak about systemic issues. Momma didn't see her parents own a business. It was more important to have stability and go get a J-O-B, period. Stability was key, so that was her mentality, which carried over to my siblings and me for a long time. I do have to tell you guys that my family has had a major generational curse broken. My sister and I are both full-time business owners, and my mom has had one children's book fully published and written dozens more. So, we have been FREED from thinking that working for someone else is the only thing that equals stability!

Before I move on from this lesson, I want to touch on what I meant earlier when I said this lesson would become a limiting belief later in life.

Before I joined the military (we will talk more about this later), I went to Wright Business School. The was one of those technical schools that teach you a trade in like 6 months to a year. When I signed up for this school, I remember calling momma to tell her. Well, this conversation did not go well. Mom was so disappointed that I wanted to go to a tech school and told me that it would be better to spend about the same amount of money and go to a 4yr university.

Now, I know momma meant no harm, and there was actually a lot of truth to what she was saying! However, at the time, I took that to mean that a tech school was not good enough. This led me to believe that the online & community college degrees I earned later in life were not good enough. Which really led to me never talking about my degrees or shying away from using my degrees in any way. To this day, there are still very few that even know I have a Master's level education. I'm shy about talking about it still because it was a part-time online course.

Do you see how allowing even a harmless seed to be planted can change the trajectory of your life? Momma meant no harm at all, and she was right. I should not have been rushing into Wright Business School because I ended up with debt and not one job to show for it, lawd! However, we have to be very careful about how deeply we allow someone else's words to take root. Because sis, it is very hard to uproot ideas about ourselves once they take hold. These ideas become strongholds in our lives that must be broken for us to move to the levels God has called us to.

My parents both taught me so many lessons, but we all know that our household is not the only life "classroom". A major part of my story takes place during my primary school years, 6-12th grade. Now, I have no plans to bore you with walking through my entire school experience. However, some of the events in my school years are an intricate part of my story, very much woven into the things I went through later in life and the person I am today, so I will touch on some of the major events and life lessons.

The Real Classroom

My memories of school before the 6th grade are actually very blurry at best. I can remember some bits and pieces, but nothing like the memories from 6-12th grade. I think that was the first time I formed meaningful relationships with the people at school so it just had more of an impact on me.

It's funny that the first thing I mention is meaningful relationships because one of my first memories of 6th grade is meeting a girl who would be my bestie for a very long time. A friend that would also be the cause of much pain in my life, honestly. Kandy was about 5'10 and what we used to call high-yellow. I was actually drawn to Kandy right away, literally from the first day of school. She had a slick mouth, and even the boys in the class were afraid of her. I don't remember exactly how, but I remember we slowly started to hang out together at recess. THEN, we discovered that we lived in the same apartment complex, so we started walking to school together too.

Not long after I met Kandy, we started to hang with Bri as well. She was literally the exact opposite of Kandy. Short as all get out, dark-skinned, long curly hair, a mouth full of braces, and quiet. Well, she was outwardly quiet but definitely had a slick mouth when we were alone! I'm still friends with Bri to this day! We had a lot of healing to do, but we made it through because we were both willing to work through it. Me and Kandy, on the other hand, we do not speak. There is no bad blood. That friendship just didn't make sense in adulthood for us.

Ya'll know I love a good lesson, and that last sentence is the premise of this first lesson: ***Stop holding on to past relationships that are no longer fruitful.*** If you are involved in a relationship of any kind that is draining you and the only reason you are still involved is out of obligation, let it go! You are not obligated to stay friends with someone just because you have known them for a long time. This goes for romantic relationships as well! Stop looking at relationships like a contract. Like you must fulfill your relationship to-do's and never let them go.

No ma'am! Stop ignoring the instructions God is giving you to let that relationship go. Someone needs to read this right now because it's coming out of nowhere, so this is your sign. Stop ignoring God. The longer you stay in a relationship that is no longer in alignment, the longer you are blocking your breakthroughs. The people you allow into your space will be extremely important as you move to your next level. Everyone is not supposed to come. More on that later…

So, back to the girls and me. My friendship with them is very important because it is part of what helped me survive and what broke me again at one point.

Our friendship provided the distraction I needed

from the pain I was feeling inside during the survival mode. My inside pain was screaming most of the time, but being around Bri and Kandy made me feel like things were normal, and I got to laugh like I had never laughed before. I mean, we became known for laughing at everything. It didn't matter where we were if something was funny...we would be on the floor laughing! I'm literally cracking up as I write this thinking about some of the times we laughed about literally nothing! They were the first people I opened my heart back to during this time, and it was really nice. Some of the best times I've ever had in my life. Now, I know some may say, "It was a childhood friendship; it's not that deep". Well, I was a child with the emotional intelligence of a 40yr old LOL. I was *very* in tune with my feelings and how my feeling made others feel. So it was that deep for me.

I think the thing that attracted me to Bri in particular was that she was also the product of a broken household and her mom was a single mom. So, it was like, even as kids, our traumatized spirits comforted one another, and I truly believe that bond is partly why we are still friends. I got to watch Bri eventually walk down the aisle with her father, over 20 years later, only months after my own daddy passed away. Little did we know that trauma would bond us once more when her dad passed just a year or so later.

While Bri and I were getting so close, my relationship with Kandi changed. We were still friends, but I started to see something in her that wasn't really a friend to me.

The things she had, like a present dad, a house (they finally moved out of our apartments), two parents in the household…these things started to feel like her excuse to be pretentious. Now, I can be real and say that some of that feeling could have been childhood jealously on my part.

However, I know me, and I know how I am…I am not like that. I have always been the person to jump up and down with actual joy when someone I care about succeeds. So, I truly don't believe it wasn't jealousy. It was her condescending tone, her laughter at situations that made me cry, her quickness to randomly cut me off over the years, and her unwillingness to talk about anything that didn't directly involve pumping her ego. I know some of ya'll know Kandy very well. You may not know her directly, but you know her spirit because she is your current "frenemie". Ya'll are friends, but one slick sentence away from walking out of each other's life again for the 15th time.

Like I said earlier, me and Kandy do not have any hard feelings now, but chile did she teach me some lessons! Besides teaching me the lesson of letting people go when your season with them is over, Kandy also taught me two other key Lessons:

#1 Don't give anyone permission to treat you badly

I don't remember when, but at some point, I gave

Kandy permission, to start mistreating me. It started as small jokes about the way I was dressed or how I had my hair done. Then it slowly morphed into joking about the "ghetto" apartments I lived in (the very same ones she moved out of, mind you), and even the way I looked. Now, this was all wrapped and deceitfully packaged as "joking around", but it was tearing away at my soul, and I actually started believing her insults. Looking back now, I recognize that I was in an abusive relationship. I loved Kandy as a dear friend, so I allowed the joking, but the little girl that had stared into that mirror and told myself how ugly I was, was believing every word of her jokes.

It is imperative that you never let anyone, I don't care who it is, start to abuse you verbally under the premise of "jokes". This is where it starts, and I'm telling you, regardless if you see it or not, it's affecting you. It's like someone slowly chipping away at a piece of wood until it breaks in half. Sometimes the person may not even realize what they are doing, but I truly believe sometimes they do. Some of these people have a keen eye to see pain, and they will go after it. But they won't hurt you blatantly because they want to keep you around to keep chipping away at you. Check out this golden gem:

> *Physically chopping wood is a stress reliever. This is the satisfaction abusive people get when they are chipping away at the target of their abuse. Don't*

let the fact that they want you around flatter you! They want you around for them, not because they care about you.

#2 Never over-admire anyone

This one is HUGE, and I believe learning this lesson early on was a life-saver for me. I don't know if you could tell, but initially, when I spoke of Kandy, it was with admiration. Because I truly did admire her. I admired her wittiness, her ability to intimidate and stand up for herself. I admired that she was ok with who she was regardless of what others thought. I think part of me imagined that's how I would've been without my trauma.

So, I allowed my admiration for her to dictate our relationship. I chose to let her run the show, really. If she was mad about something, so was I. If she hated someone, so did I. Honestly, I think Kandy had that effect on many people, Bri included. It was as if we were her minions at one point, and that's not easy to admit. So, the lesson here really is that admiration is ok, but too much admiration can be dangerous. Too much can keep you stuck in a place someone else wants you to be. It can mean you allow someone to abuse you and sway your thoughts about yourself. Too much admiration can have you no longer listening to God but hanging on to every word of your favorite coach!

Someone needs to read this. Do not get caught up

over-admiring or worshiping ANYONE or ANYTHING but God. No one is allowed to abuse you, no matter how much you admire them.

This section of the book is very important to me because the way that my "friend" Kandy treated me set the stage for much more pain during our high school years. Because I had allowed Kandy to strip away my armor with her sly abuse, I went into high school completely ill-prepared!

The mental abuse I went through in high school with some of my peers stayed with me for a VERY long time. Actually, I just released some of it in 2020 when I stopped abusing alcohol to cover all of my pain. Let me tell you when you no longer have a numbing agent, surgery hurts like heck! When I finally faced a lot of the hurt from this time, it saddened me to actually realize what I let go on with Kandy for so long. Even after we were adults, I let her treat me like I was lower than her. I thank God for waking me up and helping me truly let that relationship go.

High school was full of new levels of trauma. I experienced what it was like to deal with the death of a close family member. One of my beloved cousins was shot and killed in his home. The whole night was devastating and changed their family and ours forever, but that is not even close to my story to tell. However, I mention this incident because it was the first time I can remember questioning God. I asked him that night why he would allow my cousin to die, and I don't remember an answer from him. The truth is, I wouldn't have heard the answer even if he did give one. I asked him the question, but I had already decided I was angry with him and would never forgive him.

High school was also the first time I endured identity trauma (not being black enough for the black kids to really make friends with me, but not good enough for the rich white kids either). It was the first time I experienced what it felt like to be used sexually. My first sexual partner at age 16 had sex with me, then brought a big bouquet of balloons and flowers to school for another girl the next day for Valentine's day (and, of course, Kandy and Bri laughed right along with everyone else like it was the funniest thing in the world).

The balloon incident and their lack of respect for me is one of the most hurtful things I can remember about high school. I'm not sure if they knew the boy was my first full sexual partner, but it was extremely hurtful. It felt like I was always the laughing stock about one thing after another with boys around that time. After the balloon incident, I had another incident with a boy that told the entire school I stunk. I mean, these stupid childhood things were happening on the regular, and it just built up to a point where I didn't want to be around any of them anymore. And to be completely 100, it was the fellow black kids that were the source of much of my trauma.

So, I retreated. I started to hang with the "gothic" kids, even dated and had sex with a boy that wore eyeliner and long hair. I was tripping, LOL!! But I was really just in search of something new. Something that didn't feel as painful. Once I had sex with the gothic boy, he told everyone, so I retreated from that crowd and started to hang with the "skaters" as we called them. Do you see how my school was VERY divided?

Honestly, the skaters were the most welcoming group of people I turned to in high school! I don't know if the weed and pills made them more chill, but listen, I got along *very* well with them. Even after high school, I stayed in that crowd. This crowd is what brought me my first boyfriend, JJ. JJ was an older white boy with long, silky, brown hair, about 6'3 and built like a stick. I met him at 16, fell in love, basically moved in with him about a year later, and he was my WORLD for 3 years.

The JJ story is a whole book in itself, so I've got a little section reserved for him in the next chapter. But I want to leave this chapter with another important lesson for you. And the lesson is:

You become who you are around the most. No matter how much you may tell yourself that you can keep relationships with people after you have changed, you are wrong. Yes, some people you are called to minister to, so I'm not saying you need to drop everyone like a hot potato. However, you cannot get to the top of where God needs you with weights holding you down. You have to release the people that were only supposed to be in your life for a season! Some of you are holding onto relationships too long. You should have released that a long time ago, but you are letting fear of the unknown stop you. Well, fear is not of God, and he is waiting for you to cut the dead fruit to allow you to grow. Everyone in your life is not destined to go to all levels with you. You have to be ok with releasing people. It does NOT mean they are bad people! Change that mindset, and maybe that will help you release them. They are not bad people. They are just on a different path, a path that is not in alignment with yours.

Those friends of yours that have chosen to start dabbling in Crystals and Tarot cards, release them. They are not the people you need to be around while God is trying to elevate you to new levels in his Kingdom. Those friends that want to ask you every weekend to go to the bar even though they know good and well you quit drinking, they can't come with you to your next level! You are moving through heavenly levels, and God is ready to accelerate you, but you are steady holding onto relationships that are completely out of alignment. Release those relationships right now, and see how much of a breakthrough you get! Be mindful of the mindsets of the people you let advise and influence you!

Lesson 3

HOW DID I GET HERE?

Have you ever been in a place in your life when you suddenly think, "how did I get here"? Well, chile, this chapter is a whole "how did I get here" moment in my life! It takes place during a time in my life when I was so broken, so lost, and in so much pain that I just turned to the most unusual places for comfort. Well, I didn't know it at the time, but I was exactly where I was supposed to be. You see, everything I'm about to tell you is all a part of a journey that I *had* to be on to be here telling you all of this!

This part of my story that is so dark makes the testimony at the end even brighter! This is why you cannot be afraid to tell your story. Your story is someone else's blessing, don't keep them from that! So, let's get into this part of my life that I'm pretty sure will shock most of you that don't know me personally!

It starts with a boy

I feel like when people say that, you just know it's going to be trouble! The boy I'm referring to is JJ, who I mentioned briefly in the last section. He was actually the love of my life for about 3 years, and I can honestly say that he taught me a lot in our time together. He was about 2 years older than me. Of course, that was part of the appeal for me. I, like every 16 year old girl, thought I was super mature, so it was natural for me to gravitate to an older boy. And of course, I had ALL of the bragging rights dating an older boy who had a car, his own apartment, and a full-time job! Girl, in my eyes, he was the best man I could ever have. I loved him so much. I would recognize later that I idolized him more than loved him, which is a dangerous place to be.

This boy was unlike anyone else I had ever know in my life. He had a boldness to him that could be very hurtful to me. In my family, we tell each other the truth, but it always has a little bit of sugar on top! JJ wasn't like this AT ALL, and that was very hard for me sometimes. While I appreciated his honesty, the way he was sometimes took me back to the situations with Kandy. It was not uncommon for him to tell me that my hair was out of place, or my clothes didn't match right, or I had on too much makeup. I would always be extra careful about how I looked before he picked me up. Now, this seems like something that should've been a red flag, but nah, I was all in. It was like I was under his spell!

JJ and I moved so quickly with things. By the second trip to his house, we were in a full-blown sexual relationship. I was going over to his apartment pretty much every day after school, and all we ever did was have sex. After a while, the trips to his house came more frequently, and I was spending less time at home. I was cutting classes to go to his house, staying there until like 1 or 2 am sometimes, then going home to sleep. At the time, my mom was working late at Walmart, so I don't think she realized just how much time I spent there. By the time I was a senior, I was pretty much living with JJ. I had clothes there; we went to the grocery store together, like, we were playing house for real!

To this day, I'm really unsure of how much momma knew about all of this. She knew I was dating JJ, but I don't think she realized how much of an adult relationship I was in with him. I definitely don't think she knew how in over my head I was with this guy. Looking back, I know I was not ready to enter that kind of relationship at such a young age. I still had massive daddy issues, and I was filling that void with this relationship. At this time, I desperately needed someone in my family to notice that I was not ok. I needed my mom or my sister to ask me what was going on with me and notice that I was in over my head. This becomes very obvious in this next part.

This next story is one only my immediate family have ever heard. Others know a wide view of what happened because of the scar it left, but very few know the actual events that took place.

A Very Dark Day

I'm sure you can tell by my use of the word "scar", that this story is one of attempted suicide. So, if you are triggered by this type of thing, there is your warning. I'm not writing this book to tell a surface-level story that withholds things that may not make me look the greatest. I'm writing it to tell you the absolute truth and help you achieve a breakthrough!

So, after JJ and I had been dating a while, I was in my senior year, and things were getting "heavy". It seemed overnight, things just changed and suddenly, there were people around who were doing MAJOR drugs. Everything from cocaine to pills, alcohol, and even heroine were around all the time. Literally it's crazy to think I was sitting there having a casual conversation with people while they were prepping all of the fixings to smoke or shoot up heroine. I never personally tried any hard drugs. I had seen too much from daddy that drugs and even alcohol at the time scared me.

This spike in drug users hanging around came because JJ had started to sell drugs himself. He started with small bags of weed, moved to selling ounces and pounds, then transitioned to selling coke and crank as well. JJ was not a heavy drug user, but he did smoke weed and dabbled in other things, except heroine.

As the drugs and drugged-out people hanging around became more and more a part of our lives, things with JJ and I changed as well. I actually took a step back from drugs (I had a bad trip on laced weed and quit for a while), so I became sort of the group's outsider. And of course, as I stepped back, another girl that was always hanging around, his Ex-girlfriend, in fact, was ready to step forward. She grew closer and closer to him, and the closer they got, the smaller I felt. You see, I was doing that "cool girlfriend" thing and acting like I was ok with their friendship when it was literally eating me up inside!

If I'm honest, I felt that I couldn't react because I would be labeled as the crazy black girlfriend. During this time, there were many off-handed racial jokes that some of the white boys liked to tell. Things like snapping their fingers, rolling their necks, and saying "girlfriend" to me… as if I had ever acted like that a day in my life. You guys know what I'm talking about. The things that sometimes make black women afraid to be themselves in a room full of another race!

One night, I went over to JJ's house unannounced. I can't remember why, but I just had a bad feeling that something was going on. I rolled up to his apartment and knocked on the door. When he answered, I saw his ex-girlfriend sitting in the background. He let me in casually, and I acted like all was well. After a little while, I asked JJ to come into the bedroom to talk, and an argument ensued. I was so enraged that this girl was at his house, and he seemed not even to care that he was caught. I felt like an idiot for being there, but I didn't want to leave. When the argument died down, I calmly told JJ I needed to go to the bathroom before I left.

Now, little did JJ know that for months, I had been stealing the single razors he had in his bathroom and using them to cut my arms and legs. Every time we would argue, every time I felt anything really, I would cut myself. Never too deep, but just enough to ease the pain. I'm sure you all know of someone who has done this, or you used to do it yourself. So many people ask me WHY I would do this, and I can never really give a straight answer. However, I think it was because my emotional pain was erased for a moment by focusing on the slight physical pain. It worked as a numbing agent for me.

So, I went into the bathroom to assume my ritual, but I misjudged just how upset and hurt I was. I was in no state of mind to be precise. As soon as I locked the door behind me, I grabbed one of his single, sharp razor blades in my right hand, and I swiftly and uncontrollably cut across my left arm. I was stunned for what felt like forever, and the blade was so sharp that it actually didn't hurt or bleed for what also felt like an eternity. But when the blood and pain did come, it came with a vengeance. It was the worst pain I had ever felt in my entire life and the more blood than I thought a body could even hold.

The next thing I remember is grabbing a towel from the shower, wrapping it around my arm, and rushing out of the bathroom screaming to JJ. He and his Ex were looking at me like I was an absolute crazy person. I don't remember what I was yelling, but whatever it was and the sight of the blood caused her to get up and run out of the door with a quickness. Once she was out of the door, JJ just kept screaming at me, "you F***ing idiot, what did you do?" He said some other choice words then said, "get your sh** and get the car".

I gathered my things in a panic with the towel now getting soaked, and we ran to his white blazer. As he started to make his way down the street, I realized he was not taking me to the hospital; he was taking me home to my mommas house! I yelled at him, "TAKE ME TO THE ER NOW"! He ignored me and the next thing I know, we were in my apartment complex, and he told me to get out.

So, I got out of the car with my blood-soaked towel, and he drove off. You would think that would've been the end of our relationship, but there was much more to come. We were back together within a week!

I walked into the house that night, and my little brother was sitting in front of the television. I asked him where momma was, and he just told me she wasn't home. It was at that moment he saw the blood-soaked towel on my arm and started to freak out! He kept saying, "what happened sissy?" and I kept telling him that I fell on a knife that was sticking up in the dishwasher at JJ's apartment. Even at his young age, I'm pretty sure he knew I was lying.

I honestly don't remember how I got ahold of my mom or if she just came home randomly, but when she did get home, she immediately rushed me to the ER. I fed her and the doctors that same story about falling on a knife. The doctor who stitched up my arm actually commented on the other scars on my arm, and I told him I had gotten cut working the shake machines at my job. Apparently, I was on a roll telling silly lies about things that night!

When the doctor was about to stitch up my arm, I told her I played volleyball and asked if I would be able to still play in our final state tournament that next week. You see, volleyball was the only thing keeping me somewhat sane, and at that moment, I realized I had just thrown that down the drain with this stunt. Volleyball was something I was just BOMB at ok! It was also the only thing in my life at that time that made me feel confident and like I was in control.

So, the doc told me she could give me stitches that would hold up during a volleyball tournament but would definitely leave a scar. Or, she could stitch me up with a finer thread, and I would be done with Volleyball for the season, but I would heal up nicely with a very light scar or no scar at all. Well, of course, I chose Volleyball. Because at the time, I NEEDED that in my life. At the time I couldn't imagine surviving the blow of not playing my very last high school game. Yes, it sounds dramatic, but that's just how much it meant to me then.

As she began to put those ugly (supposedly stronger) stitches in my arm, with every ugly strand, I knew that I would have a big ugly scar there forever.

When she was finally done, we left the hospital, and it was a very quiet car ride home. Momma is not the type to pry. She likes to let us kids come to her when we are ready to tell her the truth, even if she already fully knows what the truth is. I actually really love that about her. It creates an environment of peace. It never feels like she is pushing for information, and I appreciate that.

We never talked about that night again until I was older and had moved out of the house. I wasn't ready to tell it, and she let me have that. Thank you, momma. After that night, of course, I had to show up to school (hard to believe I was still a senior in high school as all of this was taking place) and get all of the eyes and the questions about what happened to my arm. I had it wrapped so no one could see the stitches in order to put two and two quite together, but many suspected what was going on.

I can't remember if Bri or Kandy asked me about it, but the Volleyball girls were extremely concerned. A few of the girls were not buying my "falling on a knife" story and flat out asked me if I had attempted suicide. Of course, I lied, and they moved on, but I actually hated feeling like I had to lie about it.

What I did literally haunted me for years. I still to this day have a huge keloid scar on my left arm. Up until April of 2020, it was still haunting me. I would still literally lie every time I gave blood, went to the doctor, or wore a short-sleeved shirt. During the beginning of the pandemic in February 2020, I was actually considering getting a tattoo over the scar. I had an artist draw what she thought would be a great fit. And guess what she drew. A picture of some sort of animal with horns! And ya'll, I was actually considering getting this tattoo. Ya'll see how my mind was just so clouded? Because I was allowing alcohol and pain to run my life, I could not make even the most basic of logical choices.

The only reason I didn't get that tattoo is that the first wave of Covid had started ramping up, and I was scared to go to the shop or let anyone come over. The Lord works in mysterious ways! He literally turned my fear into something that saved me from doing something I would regret for the rest of my life. He saved me from literally putting a beast on my arm. When I think back about these types of things, it reminds me that God has always been here. And this is a major lesson I want you to take away from this section of the book. **No matter where you are in life right now, God is with you. He NEVER leaves. He's just waiting for you to come home to him. And when you do, he will welcome you with open arms.**

When your friends leave

It's important for me to share this small section with you because it took me almost 20 years to get over. And I know that someone reading this has had an emotional pain that stuck around like gum on the bottom of your shoe. You think you scrapped it off, only to step down and have your sole stick to the ground again! Well, that's how this pain I'm going to describe in this short section was for me.

After the suicide attempt, somehow, Bri and Kandy started to hang out with me regularly again. You see before, we hadn't really "fallen out". We were just on different paths and didn't have much in common.

Neither one of them liked JJ, but they didn't say too much because they knew it wouldn't do any good. I was attached to him. Period.

One day, Kandy and Bri came over to JJ's house to visit me. Like I said before, I was basically living there with him at this point, and they really just wanted to be nosey and see how I was living, haha! It was an awkward encounter all around, honestly. Kandy had a habit of turning her nose up, and Bri was following her lead. We sat there all faking it for a bit, then it happened. JJ called Kisha a B**ch! Now, mind you, it was NOT in a derogatory way. Even though I know some will say, "that word is always derogatory,". I understand that, but at the moment, he was not calling her a dirty name. I don't remember the exact phrase he used, but Kandy blew up! She cussed him out and then turned around and started going off on me. I sat there and laughed because honestly, the look she had on her face made me think she was joking, even though she was going off on us. It wasn't until she stormed out of the door with Bri following that I realized she was serious. And if you remember the way I spoke about Kandy before, I knew she would use this incident to try to make my life hell. I knew she would run with it and have Bri hating me too.

Sure enough, I called her a day later, and she informed me that my boyfriend was disrespectful, I was stupid for letting him talk to women like that, and she would not be talking to me anymore. On the call with her, I acted really nonchalant…as you guys know, at this time, I was the queen of blocking off any feelings. So, I placed Kandy inside of my little heart prison where daddy was and went about my way.

The hurtful part of this story and why I felt the need to tell it has nothing to do with Kandy but with Bri. When Kandy cut me off, so did Bri. Bri was the one I felt like actually cared about me. We would have emotional or deep conversations that Kandy was not capable of. So, when Bri suddenly stopped taking my calls, stopped even really looking at me in the halls, literally cut me off, it was one of the most emotionally painful things I experienced during childhood. It made me feel as if maybe something was wrong with me. I couldn't demonize her to easily put her inside of the heart prison. Because I thought me and Bri were more than that. So once again, here I was, left vulnerable.

Once Kandy and Bri were out of the picture, I retreated further into JJ. I started skipping school even more and ended up having to take summer correspondence classes to graduate. I was just barely allowed to walk in my graduation. I remember my mom asking me why Kandy and Bri weren't talking to me, I don't remember what lie I told her, but that was a painful day without them. I had known them since 6th grade, and I still loved them both. But, JJ was my world at this time, and I could not let him go for anyone.

I'm grown now!

Once I graduated, JJ and me moved to a new apartment together. This apartment was on the other side of town, so it had a whole new feeling. I felt truly grown okayyy! I was working at an assisted living center, JJ's drug business was at a peak, and our apartment was actually quite bomb (I thought so at the time). I was literally riding with him to drop of drugs to people and didn't think anything of it. I was sitting there while the person buying would snort coke and crank up their nose to test the product. I was just there riding along as if I was just going to my man's job for the day. The lesson in this is important. And I think many need to learn it.

YOU ARE NOT ABOVE SIN! The devil is insidious. He will sneak up on you like a wolf in sheep's clothing and have you thinking things are normal that would've had you clutching your pearls a year before that! The most dangerous thing a Christian can do is assume that they are somehow immune to the enemy's tricks. This is why it's important to not give an inch. Because that inch will most definitely sneak its way into a mile real quick!

For a while, things were "normal" we were working and making meals at home, just doing what our version of good looked like at the time.

Then, like a lightning bolt, something hit our relationship and left a huge ugly mark in its wake! This lightning bolt was JJ's dark world of Pornography. Now, I know this may be a dramatic way of saying it, but you have to remember that porn was not as accessible and common back then. We were not carrying around digital devices in our pockets and purses, and the internet was slow and cheap.

This wasn't the first time I had experienced porn. I had caught glimpses of the porn shows on the fuzzy tv channels before. However, this introduction was much harsher. Now, this introduction was not voluntary on JJ's part. I had actually stumbled upon it on his computer, then of course, confronted him about it. I was actually quite hurt by it, to be honest. As a black girl dating a white man, it did something to my soul when I saw images of many blond-haired, blue-eyed, naked women on his computer screen! I know this is something many don't admit, but I felt insecure knowing that he liked to look at white women more than black women. This moment is what started to make me question if my vagina was ugly, if my areolas were too big and black, if my butt was too big, etc.

Listen, I know this is a lot, but these are the things I'm so tired of us not talking about. Yes, we are Christian women, but we are also black women! Many of us have insecurities that we never talk about because we are afraid of coming off as unholy. Well, I refuse to be yet another woman, writing another book that has half-truths and cleaned-up stories! As a brand coach, I help women regularly tell their stories through their brand. And when they begin to tell their stories passionately and authentically, their brands begin to elevate very quickly!

So if there is anything you learn from me, learn this: ***Your story deserves to be told unfiltered.*** The people that God has called you to touch in some way deserve to receive the authentic you. Never separate yourself from your story to keep the appearance clean and holy. Because let me tell you this, God loves to give us testimonies. And if he has given you a breakthrough, you have a responsibility not to keep that to yourself. You have a responsibility to share it with the world. It's all for the kingdom.

What that being said, the reason I'm telling you about this dark introduction to porn is because not even a year later, I would find myself up on a pole dancing for dollars in one of the raunchiest clubs in Oklahoma City. I know, you totally didn't see that coming! Girl, when I say God saved me, I was not playing.

Lesson 4

STRIPPER POLE TO THE FLAG POLE

Usually, when I tell people the part of my story about me stripping for a year, I get one of two reactions. Either they gasp and clutch their pearls, or they are like, "HAAAYY, go girl"! It's really crazy how everyone has completely different opinions. The pearl clutchers automatically think I was having sex for money, and the HAAAYers think I was basically partying every night. Well, both would be wrong. I was never sleeping with men for money, and life was not a constant party.

Another question many people ask me is if I was on drugs or drinking at the time. NOPE, I wasn't doing either one of those things. I never had more than one beer in my life until about a month before I quit working at the club. The night I met my Ex-husband. But I will touch on that more later. I want to tell you about how I got into stripping.

I think it's important that I don't skip over this part because it's a little uncomfortable. Because again, I want you to see the complete journey to hopefully see the complete breakthrough and experience one for yourself!

So, I mentioned my introduction to porn in the last chapter and how JJ's descent into porn negatively impacted my self-esteem. I didn't mention that while he was worshiping these women on the computer screen, I became obsessed with losing weight. I was barely eating and weighing myself every single time I went to the bathroom. The thing that made it worse was that the more I tried to lose weight, the less I lost, and the more JJ commented on how ugly I looked. Like, ya'll, he had a very mean side! He would say things to me like, "he should've known I would get fat because black women get fat in old age".

Looking back, I wonder why JJ was even with a black woman. I feel like he has many prejudices about black people in general. He told me on SEVERAL occasions that he believes black people deserved slavery and were built for it because we were too weak of a race to fight back. His logic was that there were plenty of us to fight, so why did we "allow" ourselves to be enslaved. This is the absolute CRAP he was spewing and putting into my head regularly. I thought of myself as nothing but a piece of dirt on his shoe. And honestly, he was not just affecting how I felt about myself, but the way I felt about my entire race.

I was overweight, depressed, had terrible self-esteem, and on top of all of this, I had lost my job and was completely living off of JJ and his drug business. I felt useless, and feelings of suicide started to creep back in. I had also started secretly cutting again.

So, I'm in this horrible, dark place, and one day while I was out, I don't remember where, I ran into an old high school friend of mine, Careen. Now Careen was a girl that I had met during my "skater phase" in highschool. She was still the same gal I knew back in high school! Black died hair, dark clothing, smoked week every day and could out drink any man I knew. Come to find out, Careen's boyfriend was a DJ at a low-budget strip club in Southwest Oklahoma City, Francie's. I wasn't old enough to get into any other club at the time, so she asked me if I wanted to go with her to Francie's to hang out. When we went inside, I was fascinated with what I witnessed!

I saw women of all ages and sizes walking around half-clothed as confident as ever! I was just floored by this type of confidence exuding from women, honestly. I seriously could not wrap my head around it! Here I was, obsessing over my weight and my boobs being too small (I used to be a double-A breast size), and these women were walking around naked.

I was literally hooked by the idea of having confidence like that. So, I talked to the manager right there on the spot and asked if I could work there as a stripper. Of course, he took one look and said yes. I told JJ about what I was thinking that night when I got home, and he was ecstatic about it! He actually said it was a smart idea and hyped me up about how much money I could make. Thinking back on it, he was actually quite manipulative about the situation. Once I mentioned it even slightly, he used fake flattery and guilt about not helping with bills in the past to convince me to take the job.

I showed up at Fancies' the next day a few minutes before opening, with the best bikini I had, ready to dance my heart out! They asked me if I had ever danced before, and I explained that I had done nothing but dance around the house. So, they had a few ladies show me the ropes and simple dances. Then I threw on my bikini, they opened the doors, and customers started to come in. At first, I was extremely nervous, and everyone could tell. I was up on that stage looking like a deer in headlights. I had the perfect body for dancing, long legs, a big behind, flat stomach, a knockout, really, even though I could've sworn I was overweight, at the time!

Eventually, one of the girls taught me how to do the booty clap, and after that, I was dominating! In my mind, I was the best girl there! Eventually, I gave myself the stage name Fantasia. I chose something that didn't even sound like it could be a real name. I was like I was a completely different person when I was at Francie's! I would immediately get into character as soon as I hit the door.

While my stage presence was improving over the

months, so was my self-esteem! JJ had started acting weird again and kicked me out of his house, but part of me didn't even care! I moved in with a friend, Bandy, and she was cool as long as I gave her my half of the rent. About a week after JJ kicked me out, I went back to our apartment to get the rest of my things, and he was there with none other than his ex-girlfriend again! This time was very different than the last, though. It was actually comical. I had shown up looking like one of Charlie's Angels, with my sunglasses, hair and makeup whipped and laid, and a stunner outfit. The way her mouth dropped open when she saw me is still burned into my brain.

You see, even then, there were small glimpses of who God wanted me to be. Just little moments of time would hint to what "future me" would look like. We often cannot recognize those moments when we are in their midst because we never really see our true potential. Sometimes it takes someone else's validation for us to realize just how bomb we are! I could tell by the look in JJ's eyes he was regretting every word of his breakup speech. But, I stayed strong at that moment, gathered my things, and turned around and left the apartment. But I didn't leave without a show. The sidewalk back to my car turned into my own personal runway, Okurr! I knew JJ was watching, and I treated that slab of concrete like a runway in Milan.

Little did I know that would not be the last time I strutted my heels down that particular "runway". Just a few short months later, I was back over at JJ's apartment having my first ever one-night stand!

I had moved into an apartment with a friend of mine who was kind enough not to question my stripping job and just bold enough to ask me daily how much money I made the night before. She was a nice girl, and I think my dancing was almost like a fantasy for her. She was so intrigued by it, almost as if she wanted to do it too. To this day, I wish I would've had the courage to tell her that it wasn't as glamourous as she thought. I sat there and let her believe that I was the most confident woman in the world, and glamorized being a dancer because I knew she was intrigued. It was the first time someone actually thought something I was doing was worthy of envy. So I milked it. Shame on me!

Anyway, back to this final encounter with JJ. One evening, he called me at my new apartment and asked me to come over to his house. At the time, he was still selling wholesale clothing at the Flea Market, a side gig we used to do on the weekends, and he asked me to come over and help him with the inventory. Now, I knew good and well that man didn't want me to come over to count inventory! I showered, shaved, and put on my best outfit and headed over to his apartment. When I got to his house, we actually went into the spare bedroom and started counting some inventory, but that didn't last long!

The next thing I knew, we were on the floor going at it. This was the very first time I had ever had anything that resembled a one-night stand. Even though it was JJ, it still felt like a one-night stand because I was different. Working in the club had matured me in many ways. I talked different, carried myself differently, I was a woman. Before when I was with JJ, I was still behaving like a high school girl. Now, things were different. JJ actually said, "You are different, you look so good. Why weren't you like this when we were together?" LISTEN, when he said that, I'm not sure if he meant it as a dig, but for me, it was one of the nicest things he could've ever said to me! I realized at that moment that the people you keep in your intimate spaces can make all of the difference in your life. These people are so close to you that their opinions can literally change your opinion of yourself.

There is danger in surrounding yourself with toxic people. People that are constantly talking negatively about you and do not have your best interest in mind. These "frenemies" and verbally abusive men in your life must go! There are so many lessons I could teach about the environment, but if you take nothing else away from this section, take these two lessons:

Environment Lesson #1:

Surround yourself with a variety of people. Yes, you read that right. Stop spending every waking moment with the same people. There is absolutely no growth in that. You need to be seeing different perspectives no matter how grown you are. When you are around the same people all of the time, you start to forget that there is more out there in life. You start to live in a smaller box. It's like a flower with stunted growth because the owner put it beneath a shady tree. You need to move from under the COMFORT and shade of your current crowd! Because while they may mean you no hard, they are not the only thing you need in your life.

Even with all of the emotional traumas of high school, one thing I still appreciate to this day was that I decided to associate with a variety of people. Because of this variety, I learned early on how to be comfortable in many different environments and hold conversations with a variety of people. I truly believe this ability is what helped me get many higher positions in the military later on working for high-level generals and in positions people of my rank didn't normally get access to.

Environment Lesson #2:

Seek to be in the environment of those who can elevate you. Get around people you can have REAL life conversations with and learn something! Maybe they can lend you business advice or parenting advice, or they can teach you about how to purchase your first home, etc. It's nice to just chit-chat about nothing sometimes, but if you seek to move to your next level, you need to start having some next-level conversations! You should not be the only one in your "friend group" that can talk about higher-level things like business, real estate, childcare, legacy, political issues, etc. If you are, you need to do a self-inventory of why? Is your ego too big to surround yourself with other women on your level? OOPS, I said it out loud!

Many of us women actually struggle greatly with ego. We love to say that men have egos, but men aint got nothin' on some of us! While it can be natural to cling to the superior feeling of knowing the most in the environments you are in, pride and ego are not of God, and it can actually be detrimental to your breakthrough! So if that is something you are struggling with, release it NOW!

This lesson is actually one of the major reasons my life drastically changed. I stopped being afraid, intimidated, or too full of pride to go into rooms where I was at the "bottom". I started signing up for coaching with people that I knew were way ahead of me. I started applying to be in groups that I know the members are lightyears ahead of me. I remember hearing a coach online saying, "Just get in the room". This really jolted me! It made me realize that I needed to get in the room with people that could help elevate me. People that could help me see my higher vision and what's possible.

I'm currently in a group with attorneys, financial planners, high-level coaches, etc. Most of them 7 & 8 figure earners. One lady in the room literally just closed a multi-million dollar contract! You see, I don't mind being in a room full of people at the business level I want to be one day! Some of you are so quick to get intimidated when really you should just open yourself to learning from them. Just imagine the gems these ladies drop on a regular basis when they aren't even trying. They are just literally having conversations about the daily things going on in their business, and I'm learning so much! Changing your environment will change the doors that are open for you.

The most unexpected places

With that final night together over, JJ fell off of my radar. I was happy to move on, and he really didn't cross my mind much after that. I had matured past letting anyone so blatantly emotionally abuse me. I was still dancing at the club and feeling like I was more confident than ever. I had learned all of the classic stripper moves and was basically the superstar of this raunchy club. Ya'll I'm not exaggerating when I say raunchy. One of my fellow dancers fell off some cage bars one time and fractured her arm…she was so high she barely felt it. We wrapped her arm, and she stayed on shift and kept dancing! That's how bad it was.

Never in my wildest dreams had I imagined that I would meet a man at that raunchy club! Up until I met this man, I was the "good girl" at the club. I didn't drink, do drugs, or go home with men like some girls did. However, when I met this man, things changed.

The night he came in, I was intrigued by him, so when he bought a pitcher of beer and asked if I wanted a glass, I trusted him, so I took it. I remember as I was drinking that night, the alcohol gave me one of the best feelings I've ever had. It wasn't like how many other people describe their first experience getting drunk. I didn't get sick, or throw up, or even make a fool of myself. I literally felt like I had come alive for the first time. I was confident, carried a conversation easily. I was magnetic. It was like all of the charisma that was bottled up inside me just came flooding out. People were just attracted to me that night! Not even in a sexual way, but people were just drawn to me! I made the most money I ever had and had the most fun! That night, he asked me to go back to his military dorm with him. I agreed.

Now, I know your mind is all over the place right now, thinking I left and had sex with this man. Well, first, I did NOT have sex with him that night. Two, this man I'm speaking of ended up being my ex-husband John. Yes, the plot thickens! I met my first husband dancing on a pole in a raunchy strip club in OKC. Again, proof that God does not care where you have been or what you have done; he loves us all and forgives us the moment we ask! So, back to John.

At the time, John seemed like the perfect man. He was tall, with blond hair, crystal blue eyes that you could see right through, a very strong build, and a crooked smile. He was literally someone who made my heart beat faster when

I looked at him. I'm not sure why this was my "type" at the time, but it definitely was. It's funny because as time went on, he became less and less attractive to me. But we will get there. At the time, John was fairly new in the military. He was an Airman, so he was still living in the dorm room on base.

As we approached the base and the guard checked his car decal, I had this fear that overcame me. I think I suddenly realized what I was doing.

Once we got to his room, he turned on some comedy show, and I sat in his bed while he sat on the floor. He was a complete gentleman, and I appreciated that. Working in a strip club, not many gentlemen came along. I fell asleep in his bed that night, and the next day we grabbed breakfast, and then he drove me back to my car at the club. The girls had a FIELD day with this. Of course, they all thought we had slept together, no matter what I said. But I honestly didn't mind. I was already hooked.

After that first night at the club, he would come in regularly just to chat with me. He would buy a dance, and one time he asked to have a dance with another girl and me. Now, this was a red flag that I ignored at the time. Here we were, basically dating, he was coming into the club, we were talking on the phone for hours, I was spending time in his dorm, we were going out to dinner, and the movies…but you are asking one of my friends to join in on a strip dance for you? At the time, I wasn't strong enough to say no.

I was too afraid he would think I was the jealous type and decide to leave. It had only been a few months, and already I was dangerously attaching myself to him! I was already choosing what HE wanted over what I needed. I was choosing his happiness over my values. But again, we go back to the environment. How could I, a dancer in a strip club, ask him NOT to get dances from the ladies I worked with? It's like being at a party where people are snorting cocaine, then getting mad when they offer you some! If you are going to surround yourself with mud, don't be surprised if you get some splashes on you! This little red flag, and the fact that I chose to think that John just happened to walk into that strip club randomly one day, was a true sign of my ignorance! I missed so many signs it's not even funny.

However, in true "old me" fashion, I ignored the red flags, and we continued our relationship until one day I woke up and I was basically living in his dorm room and spending less and less time at my apartment. This should be sounding familiar to you. This is the EXACT pattern I went through when I was dating JJ. We started dating, then I immersed myself into his life and slowly cut off any semblance of my own.

I'm THAT girl

Now, not everyone in John's life was excited that he was dating a stripper. Of course, his military guy friends thought it was cool, but the one girl friend always had an attitude, and his family just didn't know what to think. The funny thing is, the stripping is not what shocked the people in John's life the most about me. The fact that I was also a black woman was an even harder pill for them to swallow. His military friends, of course, pretended to be ok with it, but the slide remarks about my weave or the occasional white guys doing his best "Shanaynay" voice at me told me how they really felt.

John's mom was very passive-aggressive about it as well. She said she was ok with it but proceeded to show me every single picture of John and his white high school sweetheart when I visited her home in Minnesota for the first time. I sat there politely for HOURS as she poured over every image of this skinny, blond, white girl that she "thought her son would marry". Never once did I say a disrespectful word to her. But John definitely heard it on the way home! You see, I had been through this before with JJ's white mother too. The smile that you just know is laced with "what the heck is my son doing with you"! John's mother remained this way for the entire 7 years we were married. The only time she acted like she loved me was when I left her son.

Despite the crap from his friends and family, me and John ended up getting married just about 8 months or so after we met. There was no proposal, just a conversation on our way home from Minnesota about how this would be the best move for us because I was thinking about going into the military by this time, and he wanted to get out of the dorms. There was really no talk of love at all during this conversation. It was actually quite cold and calculated. We drove to a courthouse in Shepard, Texas, about a week or so later and sealed the deal. I say it that way because that's what it felt like. It felt like a transaction void of love or any sort of passion. Shortly after we married, we moved into an apartment down the street from the base and within about a month, John was deployed, and I was left alone with a new apartment, our new puppy, and the expectation to be a full-time adult at 19-years-old.

During John's deployment was when I decided to go to Wright Business School (I spoke about that earlier), and life was actually ok. I had my cousin Rema come stay with me, and we actually had a fun summer! Back then, deployments for the Air Force were only 3 months, so time flew by, and I grew up a lot. John came back to a wife that was just a little more grown-up than when he left. I was very proud of how I had handled myself as a new military wife. In fact, I was so proud that just a few months after John's return from deployment, I was at the Air Force recruiters office starting the process to enlist as well.

Someone asked me why I chose to go into the military, and I said it was because I needed a job, but it was definitely because of John as well. Through him, I saw the military in a different light. I got to see firsthand that, for the most part, it was like having a regular job. Or so it seemed on the surface. I thought going to the military was the only option I had since I couldn't find anything even remotely close to what I learned at WBS! At the time, I was working for a car auction lot, and it was an exhausting job, honestly. We walked around this huge lot all day in the dead of summer while the dispatchers radioed us to pick up Junkers in the lot and drive them through the auction. Many times with no AC!

So, the idea of the military seemed like a cakewalk to me, and once I spoke to the recruiter, I was all in! I had no idea at the time just how much my life was about to be changed forever when I joined the military, for better and for worse.

Lesson 5

MILITARY TIES

"**I**'m in the NAVY. I'm in the NAVY"! That's what I was told to scream over and over again at the top of my lungs for about 30 minutes straight. Funny thing, it was not a Navy sergeant that told me to do this. It was an Air Force Staff Sergeant, LOL! As I was waiting to go to Air Force basic training, my recruiter required me to attend this "mock basic training" event. So, I put on my best Old Navy t-shirt and jeans and showed up for this event. Well, I didn't realize that Military Technical Instructors (MTI's) not only love to yell, but they are full-blown comedians! My dusty Old Navy shirt was the perfect target for them.

So, this was my first real experience with the Air Force. I thought about removing this chapter, but the military has played a pivotal role in who I am as a person. I really grew up a lot, and that was not without very great highs and super dark lows. These military moments that have major lessons attached.

I'm READY!

The first of these moments actually takes place before I even left for the military. At the time, I was almost 20, and while I had signed on the "dotted line", I hadn't actually left for basic training, so I was in what's called the Delayed Enlistment Program (DEP). While I was in this program, I had to lose 20lbs because apparently, I was overweight by military standards.

So my recruiter had basically lied and put down that I was the correct weight and told me I had to lose it before I went for my final physical the day before basic training! Chile, when I tell you, I went into beast mode! I immediately started going to the gym on base and barely eating. By the time my recruiter saw me again a month later, I was about 25lbs down. I was so proud to attend the DEP pool party and show him and the other recruits my accomplishment. Well, his reaction wasn't exactly what I had expected! When he saw me, I had dressed in my best pair of daisy dukes and a top to show my new figure (yes, ridiculous); his response was saying loudly, "Damn, I told you to lose weight, not become anorexic". He and a few of the other recruits laughed, and I laughed too (to keep from crying).

Looking back at this now, it's not even that serious. But at the time, I was still fragile. Up until this point in my life, I had been through one emotional trauma after another and not dealt with literally any of it.

> *Side note: trauma looks different for everyone, especially emotional trauma. As you are reading through these chapters, you may feel like the things I'm talking about are not big. However, you must remember that when I'm telling a story, it's from my perspective at that time. So a much younger and much less healed perspective.*

So, of course, I kept that in, and everyone wondered why I decided not to swim that day. Well, it was because while they had moved on from this seemingly insignificant incident, I was questioning my entire existence, lol! The lesson here is not one that you would expect. I could say the lesson is about healing from past trauma or something about self-confidence. Well, the lesson I want to teach here is simple but hard to learn:

Don't let everything other people say about or to you take root

When we hear the things other people say about us, we choose to either take it at face value or allow it to go deeper. I tend to allow things to go deeper. I have had to learn over the years that everything does not deserve a place in the depths of my heart, but I have to constantly remind myself of that because I wear my heart on my sleeve. Now, sometimes, people give you great constructive criticism that you should listen to closely and possibly make a change. However, just because something is constructive doesn't mean you have to let it start to define who you are and how you move. You can still CHOOSE to let it take root or not.

I actually had a major mindset shift on this topic when I read the book, *The Four Agreements*. In the book, one of the agreements is "Don't Take Anything Personally". This one actually hit me quite hard because I realized that my whole life, I had been taking everything that everyone did personally. My dad was using because of me, Kandy and Bri left because of me, JJ was mean because of me, etc. I was taking everything personal! Anytime someone I loved said something about me, I believed them. I took everything they said to heart…I took it personally.

This was a very hard lesson to learn. When you have the unique ability to literally feel what other people are feeling, it can be difficult to separate what they feel from what's actually real for you.

However, this is where God comes in. Because even though I read that book, it wasn't the logic on the pages that gave me the ability to stop letting the thoughts of others be planted in my mind. It was me surrendering my life fully to God and asking him to protect my mind and soul from word curses and any other seeds that did not need to be planted! So, learn the lesson, but take that lesson back to God

ALWAYS and let him translate that into action. Because if you skip that piece, you are just out here trusting the word of a guru instead of the word of God. I promise you; there is none like him. No guru, no coach, no one.

And I'm off!

The journey through basic training for me was literally an awakening part of my life. Basic training awakened something in me I had NO idea existed. It brought out this powerful leadership side of me that had been locked away for years.

The first few weeks, I managed to stay somewhat to myself and off any major radars. I was a bed aligner, and *all* I had to do was keep the beds straight, keep my clothes folded, follow the rules to a T and just get by. Well, God had other plans, my friends! One day as I was standing in formation, minding my business as our flag bearer was getting yelled at. She was making all sorts of mistakes, and they were not happy with how she had been performing. So, suddenly, the TI yells out to the group, "has anyone here ever held a flag before or been in ROTC". Neither of those applied to me, (what a relief), so I kept my head down and waited to be called into the chow hall for lunch. The next thing I know, the TI was right in my face, asking me if I had ever done ROTC! I'm thinking, "why is this man in my face? I did not raise my hand." But, I responded, "No sir, trainee Lerohl has never done ROTC".

That answer was not good enough for him. For some reason, he wanted me (lawd). So, after a few more questions, he pulled me out of formation and put the flag in my hand. He showed me a few moves and asked me to model him. I did them apparently to his satisfaction, and within 5 minutes, I was the new flag bearer. This was a prime example of how other people can sometimes see what we can't. This is why I am such an advocate for coaching! A coach can bring things to the surface that you didn't even know existed. We can't always see what we are worth and the true talents we have. Sometimes we need someone to challenge us and bring those talents out to help us move to the next level!

Discovering The Why

Ok, some may say that being offered the flag bearer position is an awesome accomplishment, and in the end, it was, but at the time, I just wanted to crawl in a corner and melt. Even before I left for basic, John had told me to just keep my head down and get through this experience quietly. So, it almost felt wrong to be thinking about doing literally the exact opposite! I remember calling John and literally sobbing on the phone about being the flag bearer. I was completely unqualified, so every practice from 6-7 am was the worst hour of my life. Also, I was behind by about 3 weeks, so everyone else was starting to resemble a professional, and here I was struggling to pick up the most basic moves.

A couple of weeks passed, and while I was getting better, I was still not feeling too good about my skills. One day, the scariest of moments came when the Master Sergeant in charge came to watch us do parade practice. Ya'll when I say I was shaking in my boots! I completely messed up in front of this guy. So badly that he told my instructor she needed to swap me out with one of the men from our brother flight.

This was probably one of the most embarrassing things in my life. I felt like a complete failure. I had made myself right. I told myself and John on the phone daily that I was a horrible flag bearer, and I made myself right that day.

Later that evening, my instructor called me into her office to chat about what had happened. She asked me point blank if I could do it, and I said no. I told her I didn't feel qualified, and I asked if she would please replace me. She refused. GIRL…I wanted to hurt this woman. What was her problem? I said I couldn't do it!!! At that moment, she came out of Instructor mode and talked to me like a human being. She told me some of the things she had been through in her military career being one of only a few women with her previous job. She explained that she took pride in leading a flight of military women that she knew would change the world. She told me that we were one of the best flights she's ever had, and she saw the power in us. By the way, she was not wrong; the chief of my flight who became a very good friend of mine is also now a Chief Master Sergeant in the Air Force, one of the highest enlisted positions available.

I went on a week later and led my flight across the parade field with my family watching. Our final scorecard read: 100%, no discrepancies! Boss moves! And just a week before that, I had thought it was impossible to ever walk across that parade field with the flag, let alone march us to a 100% score! **But God calls the unqualified**. And he knew I needed to learn how to be in a leadership position, literally leading women to their next level. You see what he does? Even then, he was positioning me for my destiny.

So, here is the lesson I want you to take away from this section of the book:

Know your why before anything else!

When my instructor poured out her heart to me and told me why it was so important that a female lead our group, it resonated with me. HER why motivated me so much that I could literally learn weeks of flag tricks and marching within one week! Her why motivated me to do better. Don't you want your brand, your course, your framework, etc, to have that effect on people? When I talk to people about their brand, I play a little exercise and ask them why they are in their business. Then, no matter how they answer, I ask "why", and I continue to ask why no matter how they continue to answer. I keep this going until I have asked why at least 10 times. You would be FLOORED by the clarity that comes out of this little exercise. I've had women ready to change their whole business model; people cry, it's wild. We all have a reason for doing what we do. And the more clarity we can have around that why, the better we will be able to convey our message to the world. This is how you learn to truly be authentic in your brand messaging.

If you don't know your why, you are simply replicating what others are doing. That is not scalable or sustainable. Putting yourself out there as a brand or a business requires you to know this deeper why. This is what will draw people to your brand in a way that NOTHING else can. Some of you may have ideas to start a company that you have nothing to do with. Meaning you want to make a product, put it on the shelves, and collect a check. Well, sis, I hate to break it to you, but before Walmart or Target or QVC, etc., puts your product on the shelves, guess who they have to meet? YOU!

You still have to go and represent your brand to get through the door! Whew, someone needs to hear this… The doors you are waiting to open up will not open if you are trying to stay in the background. Because without the foundation of your why, no one will understand the brand and be passionate about it like you are. Never downplay the sweat equity that needs to go into building a successful brand. But that piece is for another chapter!

The Overachiever

After my experience with the flag bearer position, it was like I was literally attracting amazing opportunities within the military. I went to tech school right after basic training, and my career field at the time (ground radar) happened to be offering a deal to choose any base you wanted, stateside or overseas, if you passed the course with the highest average. Suddenly, I had all of the confidence in the world to do just that even though I had almost failed out of high school for non-attendance. Ya'll I kept my nose in my books for 6 weeks straight and graduated with a 98%. I believe I only missed one question on a test or Physical Evaluation the entire time! People were asking to study with me because they were literally floored how I was getting 100% on exams that the rest of the students weren't getting above an 80%. As a result of this accomplishment, I chose my orders, and Germany was first on the list!

Not only did I choose Germany because my ex-husband wanted to go there, but I also wanted to travel, and the ground radar job there was not so "gruntish". Instead of being outside in a mobile radar unit with the army, I would get to be inside an Operations Center doing flight planning and working alongside experts in lots of different airframes.

This beginning part of my military career was an ego booster! I was so confident, I looked good, people looked up to me, I was on cloud nine! It was only when I got back home from tech school that I realized life back at home didn't feel as good. John was jealous of my accomplishments and just wanted to drink and go out all of the time. At home, I felt disconnected from my friends. I realized very quickly that home wasn't home anymore.

    I was only in Oklahoma City for a few weeks or so before it was time to head to Germany for my 4-year tour. I said my goodbyes to my family. I don't remember how, but somehow I ended up seeing Kandy and Bri before I left as well. We all hung out for New Years'. I still have the photo in my office. It was nice to see them for once when I didn't feel like a loser. It was nice to be on top for once and feel like they actually respected me. You see, Bri and Kandy had also gone into the military (crazy, right)! They were both in the National Guard at the time, so they were still at home, but I could tell they respected me not only for going to the military but for going on active duty as well.

    A few days later, I said my teary goodbyes to my family and boarded that plane with John to Germany. During my tour in Germany I really found out exactly what I was made of. This literally changed everything for me. I grew up while I was there. I had some of the best times of my life and some of the worst. So much happened there, and quite honestly, that's a book all in itself, so I won't go into each detail. However, some pivotal moments just can't be left out. I want you to experience why I had such a breakthrough when it finally came.

The people and moments that change us

The one person who probably seems weird to mention in this story, but had such an impact on me , is my first commander, Lt. Col Emery. He was a fairly young guy for his rank and super nice. He actually was formally a speechwriter for the whitehouse, so you can imagine how inspirational this guy was, lol! It was like when he gave speeches, I would be literally hanging on every word. This was the first time I can remember being so inspired simply by someone talking. I grew up in the church, so I was inspired by Godly things, but this was different. This was the first time I had someone in charge of me in a work environment that inspired me to actually want to work harder. Made me want to go further and do my very best for them. It was amazing!

    The thing that changed me, though was that Lt. Col. Emery was not only a great speaker; he put ACTION behind his words. He cared so deeply about his troops, and he would swiftly reward those that cared about the mission and showed it. During his time in command, he encouraged our supervisors to put us up for awards and treat us with dignity and respect. I loved that about him. As a result, I quickly gained huge amounts of recognition! Within one year, I made "Below the Zone", a military award that basically gets you ranked up faster. After I won BTZ, I won several other awards to include an award for the entire German military community (KMC)! My name even got put up for a numbered Air Force award, one of the highest honors! Ya'll I was literally on cloud nine. I was hard-charging through the military and ready to definitely stay in for 20 years and be The Chief Master Sergeant of The Air Force! Period!

However, what I didn't understand at the time, was that no matter how good you are doing on the surface, if your foundation is weak, the big beautiful house you are building WILL fall. I was doing all of these amazing things on the outside, but I still hadn't healed from anything emotionally. So after work, I was coming home and drinking those big, strong, German beers until bedtime. I remember even taking beers with me to bed, actually. God wasn't even on my radar ya'll, and so, I fell victim to the very thing I thought I never would. I started to normalize binge drinking. I let my guard down and didn't even think twice about having one too many drinks. I rationalized my drinking because "everyone else was doing it".

I got caught up in this military culture of binge drinking. And yes, although many will never admit it, there is a huge culture of drinking in the military that is not ok. I can remember getting completely wasted in Germany with some of the people that were supposed to be watching over me. Unfortunately, many of my brothers and sisters in arms struggle with alcohol abuse, and a large part of it is because it is normalized and almost forced. If you are not drinking, you are on the outside. So, there I was, the daughter of an addict, becoming one myself. But it would be 10 years before it would really start to manifest outwardly.

The lesson for this section is simple: *Check on your strong friends too.* Check on your friends who are leaders and seem to always have it together. They don't always have it together! I was binge drinking with friends on the weekends, and they were going back to "normal life" during the week, but I was coming home every night and drinking myself to sleep, and no one had a clue.

Because I was operating as normal at work, working out, a model Airman, no one bothered to ask. I seemed perfect. I seemed strong. I worked extremely hard to become this person that no one would question. Because I knew deep down that if I showed even a little bit of what I was really feeling, the glass would shatter. Like, I may have ended up in the Air Force alcohol abuse program and military mental health as well. The things going through my head about myself as I would stand up to get awards very dark. I was also still cutting, but it was no longer helping, so alcohol became my blade. It's so hard to believe this gets worse, but it does.

Lesson 6

SENT TO SAVE

About halfway through my tour in Germany, I met my friend Carrie. Carrie was a white girl with swag, okay! She was from Cali, super laid back, and we just became really fast friends. She was married without kids as well, so we had a lot in common. I can't remember for sure, but I think maybe a few months after Carrie and I became friends, our entire squadron got orders to deploy to the Operation Center downrange. It was scary to think about going, but I felt super confident that it wouldn't be all that much different than being at the home station because we weren't forward deploying or anything. I still had not grasped the fact that danger can come in many forms. Yes, we were not deploying to the front lines, but as direct support of a front-line activity, I misunderstood just how much of an effect this deployment would have on me.

When we first arrived, the United States Military was still looking for Osama Bin-Laden. We were working on scheduling direct air support for ground troops and seeing everything going on through these huge projector screens up on a huge wall inside the Ops Center. Most days, we honestly didn't watch every move that happened on the screen. But one day, an announcement came over the loud screen that they had caught Bin-Laden's second in command. They said an Air Strike had been performed and paid off! We were all so excited. I remember feeling so good because I felt like the job we had done really helped the war effort. We scheduled flights every day, mapped out airspace, etc., but never really got to see such a direct impact like this. We all celebrated that night with our 3 drinks that were allowed, and all was peachy until the next day.

    The next day, there was a somber feeling in the air. The commander called a meeting and informed us that the wrong target had been hit. The airstrike had hit a civilian target and directly killed many civilians, including women and children. They didn't give us details, and I don't even think it was on the news (nothing gets reported to the news until after a battle damage assessment is done, then they decide if they will be informing the public). When the meeting was over, I made a b-line for the smoke porch. At the time, I was about a half-a-pack-a-day smoker of camel wide cigarettes. I smoked one, then went back inside and honestly felt like a zombie the rest of the day. I went into the bathroom and cried for a moment, but other than that, I couldn't feel anything else but stunned. You see, I felt responsible. You can't feel happy and responsible when the news is good, then just switch it off and say, "that aint my fault," when the result is bad. So in my mind, I was part of the big, bad that just killed a bunch of civilians who had nothing to do with the war.

After that day, I didn't really have that same enjoyable "important" feeling about being deployed. A few weeks later, I moved over to the Search & Rescue section of the operations center. We were in charge of coordinating the search efforts for downed aircraft and lost troops in enemy territory. Not even two weeks after me working in this section, another tragedy struck. An Army helicopter crashed downrange, and some of the soldiers onboard died, and a 25yr old man lost his limbs. It was an awful day and just reinforced the feeling of numbness. All I could think about was getting away from there as fast as possible, but that wasn't an option! Luckily, I was only allowed 3 drinks a day, so my drinking was curbed. However, I found other ways to harm myself and those around me.

I am not perfect

This is part of my story that I have not told anyone out loud. The only people who knew were the people deployed with me to witness it, and still they didn't even know the entire story. There are those that I've told bits and probably untrue pieces to. So, me telling you this right now will be the first time the entire truth will be out. Now, forewarning, I'm sure I won't be your favorite person as you read this story, which makes me nervous, but I promised to tell my full story and not hold anything back. Telling your story doesn't just involve telling the parts that make you the hero!

So, it starts with a boy again. It seems like a lot of my stories do. Even as I sit there and write this, I notice a pattern of jumping from one dysfunctional relationship to another. I guess that dysfunction started with my dad first and continued from there.

So, while I was deployed, a young man named Noah just swept me off of my feet. There, I said the first hard statement, so now I can get into this story. He wasn't my usual type, but he was just the prettiest thing to me at the time. He was just slightly taller than me, brown hair and brown eyes, and had sort of an Italian look about him. He was white but had that slightly olive skin that made me think he definitely had some other mixtures in his bloodline. One day while Carrie and me were having our allotted 3 drinks at the deployed "bar" venue, Noah walked straight up and sat down at the table next to me. He asked our names, introduced himself and began talking to us. Now, I cannot remember for the life of me what we talked about, but I know this man captivated me. His whole attention was on me. He treated me like I was so beautiful, and it really shocked me to my core.

I was open to flattery because I'd literally never had

it before. Even with my husband John. We talked all night, I did tell him I was married, but that did not seem to really matter to him. He was going to have what he wanted. That should've been a sign for me to run the other way, but for some reason, it made me even more interested.

Noah and I moved fast and quick. Before I know it, we were emailing all day at work (we did not have cell phones, back then, people barely even used cell phones over there), we were meeting up every night to have drinks, and our conversations were going on until the wee hours of the morning.

Slowly our conversation turned to a more sexual place, but it wasn't like let's have sex type of thing. It was more of him telling me how I should be treated and pretending to care that I wasn't getting what I needed from my husband. Now I know it was really all just a plan to get in my pants, but hey, at the time, I was eating it all up. So, while this emotional relationship is going on, I had started to basically ignore John. It went from me crying and begging to talk to him because he ignored me to me barely even reaching out to him. And miraculously, he noticed.

He started to email and say things like, "why haven't you tried to call me?" To myself, I was thinking, dude, really? You see, a few weeks before I left for my deployment, John had a conversation with me and told me that he felt we were just meant to be friends. He told me he was not attracted to me anymore and had no romantic feelings for me. This absolutely crushed me. At the time, I was in the best shape of my life, I thought. I was working really hard to look good even though I was drinking my tail off, but I thought looking good meant being skinny at that time. Because that's what John's standards were. So, imagine the shock when he tells me that he's not attracted to me!

So, needless to say, John was starting to get suspicious that something was going on. He knew me, broken me, and he knew that, no matter what he had done, I would never just ignore him unless there was someone else. So, you know what this man had the audacity to do?! Without telling me, he went to see my commander. Mind you, nothing physical had happened with Noah and me at this time. We were just talking a lot, and John didn't even know about him. He just knew I was ignoring him and was starting to get annoyed by it. So, he visited my commander and asked him to bring me home from my deployment! Of course, my commander told him that was not possible, but John planted a seed within my squadron that made them never look at me the same. He tarnished my reputation.

These people had the utmost respect for me, and in one moment of anger, he went into my place of employment and ruined that. While they did not bring me home, they did start to watch me like a hawk. For those of you that don't know, it's against the USMJ (Uniformed Code of Military Justice) to cheat on your spouse. So, while I still had not been physical with Noah, I was being watched very closely. My supervisor, Major Candy Saini, told me about John's visit to my commander and asked me flat out if something was going on. I lied and told her nothing was happening… in my mind, it wasn't a huge lie because I hadn't slept with Noah. I could tell she didn't believe me. Apparently, John had put on a great show! He had cried in the office and everything. This man that told me weeks before I left that he wanted to just be friends, wasn't attracted to me, sat in my commander's office, and cried about me ignoring him. Chile, I cannot.

So anyway, even with all of this tension building with John, I was still full steam ahead with Noah. I was caught up with him in a way that could withstand all of the madness going on. I had chosen to lie and whatever else to keep this thing going with him. So, as things steamed up with Noah and me, things took an even more major turn with John. One evening, I called my mother, and she informed me that John had called her saying I was cheating with some guy in the desert.

Listen, this made me madder than anything ever had at the time. My mom had written me an email that said all of these things about not letting the enemy pull me away from a good man and everything. Meanwhile, I'm thinking, John is not a good man! He treated me like the trash strip club he found me in for years. Now, I will tell you right now that I was upset with my momma at that point. However, I DO see now that she was reacting from not only John's lies, but the LIES I had been telling her for YEARS!

I was hurt by my mother at that time, because it felt like she chose him. But really, she just didn't have the full story. I had led her to believe we had the perfect marriage, so she was reacting with that impression in mind that I had created. I told her the story years later, and she did apologize. She also told me she would never again take the other side, and that feels good. I love that she made that vow to me because I need her. I need to know that my momma always has my back even when I do mess up.

So, again, all of this is going on with John, and I'm still in a full-blown emotional relationship with Noah. Now, I do have to mention that I was not calling this a relationship at the time. I did not have the wisdom I do now. I honestly felt like because I hadn't slept with him, I wasn't doing anything all that bad. I knew I was falling in love with him, but it still didn't feel wrong to me then because I was basing everything on sex. All I had known from a man was that sex is what meant we were in a relationship. From the time I became sexually active, that's all men seemed to want from me, so I never associated talking with someone as being in a relationship.

So, because I was only talking with Noah, it didn't feel like an actual relationship. Until playtime was over one night. This night, I saw the forwardness in Noah in a different way. We had managed to find some alone time in the wee hours of the morning. Both of us worked different shifts, so it was rare that we were actually able to hang out in person. Up until this point, we would meet every now and then, but much of our relationship was happening over email. Well, this night, we met up in person at an abandoned track in the compound. We talked, and as the night/morning went on, Noah got closer and closer to me, and we kissed. Now, I know this is sounding super juvenile right now, but it was a pivotal moment because it was the moment things drastically changed in our relationship. For me, I felt uneasy because it now felt like I was officially cheating on John. Also, something just didn't feel right in my spirit. I thought it would feel really good. In fact, I was looking forward to our relationship taking this turn, but I almost felt sick in that moment.

I hadn't been to church in YEARS at this point and wasn't even thinking about God, but he was definitely talking to me that night. I felt physically sick and told Noah I needed to go back to my room. Of course, he was super confused, but I just needed time to process the person I was becoming. I was literally a cheater now...that's all I could think about. So, I went back to my trailer and actually sobbed for what felt like hours before I fell asleep. When I woke up and checked my computer, I already had an email waiting from Noah, asking if I was ok and requesting another meet-up. Ya'll he was not playing any games, ok! And this time, he took it even further and asked if I could meet up with him in his room because his roommate would be gone. My spirit almost jumped out of my chest when I read that. I was a little hurt actually because I started to see him as a man for the first time. A man that just wanted to get in my pants just like everyone else always had.

So, of course, I told him no way…NOT! I agreed to go to his room that evening and hang out with him. I don't know if I mentioned that Noah was in the Navy, not the Air Force, so their trailers were on the whole other side of the compound. A side I would have no reason to be visiting, so not only was I going against my better judgment, but I was going to have to sneak to the other side of the compound without anyone watching me, finding out!

Side note, I feel like someone needs to hear this. No matter where you are at in your walk with God, he still cares about you and will STILL send his Holy Spirit to talk with you and warn you of things. Don't ever think that you are alone, and trust your intuition. That is Holy Spirit trying to protect you. God is not a respecter of persons; he loves us all the same. So, don't think that if your walk with God is not perfect right now, he doesn't care. He cares deeply for all of us and will try to talk us out of situations that will harm us.

So, here I am, getting ready to go over to this man's room. This stranger that I had known for literally about a month or so. I was going to be alone with him in his room in trailers I was unfamiliar with. Sounds like a bad movie starting, and I'm the stupid one you are yelling at through the screen to RUN! Well, I did not run away; I ran headfirst in. I had committed to going, so I was going. And, I went.

The encounter was fairly brief. I got there, and when I walked through the door, he grabbed me and started to kiss me roughly. I asked him to calm down, so he did. We sat on the bed, and he started up again, this time, I honestly didn't feel comfortable to say stop, so it kept going. The next thing I remember, he was on top of me being extremely loud (even though it was completely illegal what we were doing), and he was holding both of my arms above my head. I remember thinking he was the strongest man I had ever been with. I looked at his sailor arms and thought, "there is no way I could move if I wanted to". He continued, I got absolutely no pleasure from it, and when it was over, I put on my clothes he had torn off like we were in some romance novel, and I said, "Ok, I'm going to go".

He looked at me strangely, and I walked out. When I left that trailer, I felt so dirty. I knew pretty much everyone else in the trailer had heard what happened in his room because the man was literally yelling with every thrust! So, not only was I feeling dirty for the actual act, I was feeling embarrassed. The other feeling I had and one I don't talk about EVER, was a feeling of violation. Now, I KNOW what some of you are thinking…I'm definitely no victim here. I recognize I was an adult and part of the decision to have sex. However, I wanted to scream several moments during this encounter, but my voice felt muted. I had an actual feeling of fear when he was on top of me. I felt like if I screamed, this could turn even more violent than it already was (if you couldn't tell, he was being extremely rough and had me pinned down). At that moment, even though I didn't yell NO like you are supposed to, or even ask him to stop, I felt like I was being violated. Everything gentle about this man turned dark and ravenous that night. I was shocked.

I do want to say that I in no way want to make it seem like Noah forced himself on me. I just felt I needed to describe this encounter in detail because I know other women have had similar encounters and may be feeling alone. Like, it's mutual sex, but not really. It's hard to describe, but hopefully, talking about it will touch someone's heart and let them know they are not alone in their feelings. ***The real lesson in this is that you CAN say NO during any sexual encounter that makes you feel uncomfortable.*** Even if you are with someone you love and you chose to be there. If something is not sitting right with you and feels off in any way, it's ok to say stop. At this moment, I felt helpless, and that is not ok.

After that night, things were not the same with Noah and me. I was disgusted but pretending to carry on as normal because that's what I did at the time, and he had gotten the sex he wanted, so he was mostly over the whole thing as well. He left a couple of weeks later, and of course, we had this dramatic goodbye at my trailer room window. He said we would keep in touch, but he slowly stopped answering my emails, and eventually, I saw through My Space that he was in the arms of another woman. So, the romance was over, and I was jolted back into the reality of John. I haven't mentioned him in a few pages or so, but there was still a ton going on back at home in Germany as well.

Shortly after Noah left, John emailed me to inform me he was now dating a German girl. Part of me was upset with him and hurt that he had caused such a stink, ruined my reputation at my squadron and everything, then turned around and started "dating" someone as well. I think it felt more like a violation also because she was in my house and riding around in our car. It was hard, but I knew I had messed up too, so I really couldn't say much. Carrie was convinced he was dating this lady before we even left!

I didn't know (and still don't know) what the truth was, but I know a bigger part of me didn't care. I actually started having conversations with John about his new relationship. He sent me images of the girl, told me about their dates to the Landsthul Castle and the movies, it was strange ya'll. It was like I was absolutely numb to anything he was doing. I creeped the girl on My Space a little bit, but honestly, it felt like my love was gone. And to be even more honest, I never got it back.

Lesson 7

DOORS TO DIVORCE

The military is not the most conducive environment for any marriage. Let's just be real. Not only do families have to endure extended periods away from each other, but the absolute stress of the job can be overwhelming! The psychological warfare that goes on is unreal, and many people outside of the military don't realize it. By the time I got home from this deployment, I was drained. I literally didn't care about what happened with my marriage, and I wasn't too thrilled about continuing my job either.

When I got home from deployment, I started inquiring about cross-training into another career field. I had tried long enough to be this technical gal, then this tough gal who helped rescue task forces, but listen…I was tired.

After looking for new jobs for a while, I landed on one that seemed perfect! Air Force Flight Attendant! Chile, when I saw that job listed and the description said I would be flying around with our nation's top leaders, I was sold!

Reflecting back on it, I definitely believe I was looking for something "high level" to get that feeling back I had before my name was tarnished, and all of this crap that had happened during my deployment.

So, I gathered up all of my research about the job and took it to my supervisor. Do you know that she laughed when I said I wanted to become a Flight Attendant? She was an intelligence officer and quite honestly, super snooty. She sat me down and told me that Flight Attendant was "below" me, and I would be wasting my intellectual talents to go fly around the world cooking and serving people. Now, after having done the job, I know she was DEAD WRONG! There was nothing "low level" about flying around with the Secretary of Defense to countries some have never even heard of, going to the Pentagon to coordinate trip details with top-level officials, and obtaining visas and other important paperwork for dozens of crew members each trip. Not to mention this job led to me becoming the Resource Advisor for the flying squadron that I was a part of, handling more funds than this Captain had probably ever even thought about.

The lesson is: *Never let someone else's fear stop you from going after your dreams!* Yes, you read that right. I truly believe this Captain laughing at me about taking a job less "intellectual" had her own fears around doing the same thing! So she was projecting them onto me. Really she was envious that I was brave enough to follow my dreams instead of being tied to something I thought made me look smarter! You see, she forgot that about a year before this when I met her for the first time, she told me a story about how what she really wanted to do was be an attorney. However, she was afraid to leave her intel officer career because she came from a family of intel officers. So, I am very sure that she was projecting! But thank goodness I didn't listen to her, or my life would've taken a whole different turn. Because the choices we make dictate the life we lead! I heard that phrase on The Renaissance Man movie when I was younger, and I still remember it today.

Sometimes it's not easy to look at your life 10 steps ahead. But it is so important that you do! You must be thinking about your life through the lens of longevity. So, all of that said, I did end up taking the Flight Attendant job. And I'm glad I did. I'm glad I listened to the still, small voice in my heart that knew this was my next move. When I interviewed for the job (one of the only jobs you have to interview for in the Air Force at the time), many of the Flight Attendants told me that the job could be hard on marriages.

They told me to keep in mind that I would be gone a lot or flying without much notice, and that has been known to cause a strain on marriages. Still, I went for the job. Because like I said, I honestly didn't have much love in a passionate way for John, and we were pretty much just going through the motions by this point. However, my taking this job was honestly the nail in the coffin of my and John's marriage.

Before I began flying, I had to go to what is called Survival School. All Air Force flyers have to attend this training along with Aircrew School. By the time I got back from all of that, John and I were just used to living two separate lives. I was gone about two weeks out of each month, and the more I left, the further apart we drifted. Our sex life was non-existent. I'm talking like 6 months between sexual encounters. And much of that was him flat-out rejecting me when I would try anything.

I did try to make our marriage work in other ways. I even went as far as to do all of the papers for his Bachelor's degree. We used to always joke that I earned two degrees while in the military! Ya'll, I was trying everything to keep this marriage from falling apart. But it wasn't enough. So, I was on every trip almost that went out of our squadron. I was flying as much as possible, and as I was flying around the world, doing things I could only ever dream of, our marriage deteriorated. I made a conscious choice to put myself before my marriage. For once in my life, I chose ME and not the man in my life at the time. Finally, I chose to do something that would elevate me, instead of something that would elevate him. Many times as women, we hide behind our obligation to be submissive to our men. We use that as a way to stay small and never really step into our calling.

Well, I want you to learn this lesson: **You were not made to be small. You were not made to be overshadowed**

by anyone or anything. You were made in God's image to shine through and be a beacon for the people you are called to serve. When you keep yourself small, you are not only doing yourself a disservice, and you are also robbing those people that need your gifts. So, no more playing small!

So, while I was elevating and deciding to chose myself…Unbeknownst to me, John had begun a long-term sexual and emotional relationship with his junior military co-worker. Girl, when I say this plot can't get any thicker, lol! I found out about this affair as I was paying the phone bill one day. This was before texting was normalized, when we used to get charged extra for every single message. So, as I was going through this phone bill, I saw tons of text messages, some even images and videos with a number I didn't recognize. It was peculiar to me, but I didn't immediately think about him cheating.

I honestly just thought he was talking to someone about work or something. As I began to research the communications further, I noticed many of the messages were in the wee hours of the morning like 2-4 am. THAT is when it struck me that this was not work talk. This was an affair. Actually, my immediate thought was that this was him addicted to a phone sex operating company or something. For some reason, my mind was resistant to going back to what we had been through before with the German girl, Noah, and all of that drama! I refused to believe he was actually in a relationship. So, I decided to call the number and see who it was.

What I heard on the other end was shocking. It was his co-worker Angie whom I knew very well. Angie had been over my house, to our birthday parties, smiling in my face for years, and all the while, she was in a full-blown relationship with my husband. When I asked him the details…yes, I tortured myself with wanting to know when, how often, were they in love, etc. And John was very open about it. He told me that they were in love and planning to move to Florida together if he could get orders. He said they had been together for over a year and would meet up in our home when I was out of town. Then he said something that hurt me more than anything else. He said that they would meet up in parking lots and have sex when I was home from trips.

Like times when I thought he was running to the store and it was taking a bit longer than usual, he was having sex with this woman in the car…our car! This particular act of sneaking around was the most damaging to me. It literally left a wound I had to heal from about men taking too long at the store or to run errands. We all know the small cuts can sting way more than larger wounds! This small thing that he did made me a very suspicious person. I mean, I had no earthly idea this was going on for over a year.

Needless to say, John and I decided to end things for good after that. He deployed like a week after I found out about the affair, and during the beginning of his deployment,

I filed for divorce. I refused to stay with someone out of obligation. It wasn't fair to either one of us. We were both in total agreement about the divorce because we knew it had been a long time coming. We were living in two different worlds at the time. So, it was easy to say goodbye to each other. The hard part for me was saying goodbye to the life we had built. The house we bought together, the dogs we had together, his family, my family's attachment to him, our mutual friends. These were the ties that were difficult to break. The things that really didn't even matter suddenly mattered the most.

There is a major lesson in what I just said. A lesson that can be applied in your business or personal life:

You are not obligated to stay the course with anything that is not working for YOU! If a business or personal relationship or collaboration is not working for you, you are allowed to let it go.

•*__Branding tip:__* What worked in one season may not work in the next! You having an outdated, DIY website was ok when you started, but now that you are trying to get bookings at a higher level, now that you are being asked to speak on stages with game-changers…that is not going to work! Maybe the graphic designer who was able to execute low-level graphics for you when you first started isn't the same one you take to the next level!

You have a message to give, and you can't give it if your visual identity is not attractive to the people who need to hear it. Stop operating as if you are still at your first level when you know good, and well God is trying to elevate you to the next level. You know it because you are up at night hearing his voice downloading you with ideas for elevation. You are pacing your floors and writing in your notebooks like crazy because God is literally trying to pull you into your next level, but you refuse to stop playing small. You refuse to make any higher-level commitments that will OPEN THE DOORS to the blessing. This is a mistake I see many people making in branding. They never elevate. They are still giving us those identical crusty posts with how-to tips years after they started. Where is the elevation! Something has gotten missed…and most of the time, it's their refusal to move on to their next season!

So, my journey with John ended while he was deployed. When he got back, we went to the courthouse and made it official. My eyes wanted to cry, but all I felt was freedom. Freedom from a life that was no longer mine.

Lesson 8

A SAMPLE OF SUCCESS

It's the confidence for me!

Once I divorced John, it was like things started to breakthrough in my career. I was still flying, but other opportunities were opening up like crazy. I mentioned briefly before that I was the resource advisor for my squadron. Well, this was a huge honor for me. Our squadron was one of the elite because of our mission to fly the Secretary Of Defense and our secondary mission as the "flying pentagon". The E-4B is a very advanced communications platform with a deeper top-secret mission and is also transportation for our nation's leaders. It's right up there with Air Force One. So, to be asked to manage the money for such an elite squadron was amazing for me!

I was also flying like crazy! Traveling the world. Really, I was just loving life! I was in amazing shape, I had started working out, but this time I wasn't trying to lose my butt and get skinny to accommodate a white man who couldn't understand a black woman's body! I was doing it for me! And it showed! My confidence was through the roof, and when I say every single man on that aircraft was drooling, I'm not even exaggerating, lol! I had men, black, white, and other asking me out and flirting. I know now that was the confidence I was exuding. People are attracted to confidence, and I was DRIPPING in it.

Hey lover!

Life got even better one night when I was on a mission in Barbados and met the love of my life. We were all out at the bar drinking, and this beautiful man walked in. When I tell you, my mouth dropped! Even though he had been flying with us, for some reason, I hadn't noticed him. When you are running around to get things together before a mission, all flight suits start to blend together honestly. It's like the uniform is doing its job...it makes us all blend into one vs. someone standing out as special or different, or in this case, HOT!

So, I see this man walk in, get a drink, and stand against a beam in the bar like a perfect statue carved from the most beautiful stone. He wasn't what my normal type had been (white); he had beautiful, deep olive skin, jet black curly hair, and mesmerizing biceps. Girl, I was obviously in love at first sight, and I was not shy about it! I'm literally sitting here so giddy as I write this. I went straight up to him, something I had never done before, and asked him, "why are you drinking water?" OMG, that's just what came out, and I immediately felt silly right after it. But he responded telling me that he was actually drinking Gin (foreshadowing moment…Gin would become my drink of choice and the poison of my rock bottom about 8 years or so later). Now, my husband is a very laid-back man. So, even though I was half into my 4th or 5th Vodka soda and loud as all get out, our encounter was very calm. That's one of the major things I remember about the feeling of the encounter. My spirit immediately felt calm around him. Like I had known him my entire life. Even though I thought I was so far away from God, his Holy Spirit was still right there, signaling that this man would be the next part of my life.

Our romance was fast and hot. Something straight out of a romance novel. We were traveling all over the world together, staying in some of THE BEST hotels you could dream of (we always stayed either in the same hotel as the SECDEF or very close to it), and our sex life was something I had never experienced before. Now, this wasn't just some good sex. It was different because he cared about how I felt. I had never experienced a man asking me what I want or even looking me in the face during sex. I had also never experienced a man that loved my body the way he does. He is the first man to compliment me on my butt instead of telling me it was too big. He was also the first man that didn't act like I was some freak of nature when I wrapped my hair up at night. He was the first man of color I had ever dated, and it just hit different!

If someone would've asked me years before I met my husband if I thought dating white men would affect my self-esteem, I would have argued NO to the death! I thought it was normal for me to be 5'8 115lbs and still trying to find Spanx that would hide my butt in my jeans!

I thought me waking up with ratted hair because my husband disapproved of my bonnet was normal. I thought being told that my vagina was not attractive because it was "dark" was normal. But these things were not normal. They were the result of me dating white men who refused to understand my culture and the very fabric of me. No, I don't believe all white men are created equal! But again, I'm telling you my experience with dating white men from the time I was in grade school (my very first kiss was a white boy, who also told me 2 days later that I had nig**r lips) until adulthood.

Me and my husband rarely left each other's side after that meeting in Barbados. We linked up again back at home station, and the rest is history. Maybe I will write a book about our romance one day. But, he is my rock, and he has never wavered even through all that I am about to describe in the final chapter before my full healing.

God knew that he was exactly what I needed because God knew my life was about to get much harder. You see, as I was dripping in all of this confidence and finally loving a man who truly loved me back, I was also becoming more and more attached to what had become a poison in my life. My alcohol consumption was in high gear, but I was still somehow functioning. It was not uncommon for me to be drinking until 3 am, then pouring out of bed and into my uniform at 8 am a few days out of the week. Riding to work with the windows down and gum in my mouth, hoping no one would smell my night before. I was a full adult turning into an alcoholic.

If you are sitting here reading this right now, and you've been making excuses for your alcohol consumption, I urge you to take a closer look and decide if you are on a path to overindulgence. Because it can sneak up on you. I'm not against people drinking, but I am against people not being aware of the severe consequences alcohol can have. It's a normalized drug, so be aware of your habits.

Ask yourself these questions if you think you may be overindulging in alcohol:
1. Do you wake up hungover more than every now and then? Like, twice or more per week?
2. When you go out for drinks, are you always the last one to call it quits?
3. Do you find yourself willing to give up things to drink? Like, you want to go see a movie, but you don't want to because it doesn't involve alcohol?

4. Has a close family member or friend ever mentioned your drinking?
5. Have you ever thought that you drink too much?

If you answered yes to those questions, some or all, please throttle back, love. Get a new hobby that is healthy for you.

Lesson 9

ROCK BOTTOM

Goodbye Military

My husband and I dated for about 8 months before we were engaged, then a year later, we got married. By the time we were engaged, I had decided to get out of the military. Flying was fun for a while, but it was getting old, and I just had a tug that there was something different I was supposed to do. This time was one of the hardest in my life, to be honest. No one could understand why the heck I wanted to get out after almost 10 years of service without any real plan.

I was being told by people I considered friends that I was basically stupid for getting out. I was being told that I had wasted the last 10 years of my life, and I was throwing away the rest of my life. The same people started to question my education. They said because I had earned my degree online, it wasn't good enough, and many jobs would not consider it. I was actually very scared, but the tug just wouldn't go way.

So, in August of 2012, I hung up my flight suit and said goodbye to the military. I had a "going away" (that's what we call in in the Air Force) at Buffalo Wild Wings, where a few people said goodbye, and I was ironically given an empty liquor bottle holder that came with all of the opener accouterments. They told me someone was supposed to buy a bottle to place in there, but the ball was dropped, so I just got the box. How wild is that? It just goes to show you how well I hid my life from everyone and just how tuned out the people in my life that I was calling friends were. I would definitely discover later that the term "friends" was a stretch. Many were simply work colleagues. And that is ok!

I just needed to learn how to discern that. This is what happens when you enter into ANY kind of relationship broken. You cling on for dear life even if the relationship is not that deep. Those work colleagues did not ask to be my therapist or best friend even! They were not obligated to call me, hang out with me, or deal with my raging alcoholism the next few years as I declined! They were simply colleagues, and because I was broken, I forced a title of friend upon them that they did not ask for.

On my own

The first thing I did when I got out, which was at

the urging of other people, was look for a government job. I applied for a bunch of resource advisor jobs working at a secure squadron on base. I was told that was the best thing to do, get a job using my security clearance, and something that could be 9-5 and had a good retirement and pay. This is like the party line for everyone getting out of the military when you go to TAP (transition assistance program). There is this whole program the Air Force has developed that is supposed to assist you with transitioning to the civilian lifestyle. Honestly, the most helpful part was finding out how to file for disability and use the GI bill.

These were the two things that could get me money right away, and let's be real, that's what most people need when they are transitioning. For Enlisted people, we don't learn much about investing, and when I was in, Enlisted people were not nearly as into all of this side-hustling and investing as they are now!

So, I got an admin job working in a secure building on base. It was a GS-7 position, so about $30k per year, I believe with benefits. At the same time, I was actually working evenings on an online boutique I started up. After literally searching the internet for "easy businesses to start", I came upon the idea of an online consignment boutique. It had very little upfront overhead and seemed fairly simple to get started. It was either that or a traveling Notary business, lol! So on weekends I was going around to all my friends' houses (or they came to me) and picking up all of the fashions they didn't want. I bought some racks from the thrift store and set up our spare bedroom like a closet. At first, I started selling on E-bay and was actually doing quite well! I had read the story about the Nasty Gal brand that grew rapidly on E-bay, and I was basically trying to copy what she did.

Oh, did I mention that after literally like a week, I left the cushy government job? Ya'll I'm not proud of that, but I just could not show up to the base anymore. PLUS, I had discovered that my old Commander Col. Dribble was actually the one who got me the job because he worked a few offices down. So, there he was in the office every day and actually had the nerve to tell me I should bring in candy and cookies! I felt like I was back in the Flight Attendant world, and I couldn't get out of there fast enough!

After I quit the government job to work on the boutique full time, things took a turn for the worse. My husband was still actively flying, so he was gone quite often, and I was working on my business at home. But while I was working on the business, I started normalizing having a glass of alcohol in my hand earlier and earlier in the day. And I say alcohol because I had switched from having a cocktail or wine to having Gin straight with ice around this time. To think about the damage I was doing to my body for years makes me cringe.

There were days I was grabbing a glass of Gin by 10am and making a funny joke to myself about it being 12 o'clock somewhere. This sounds very sad to me now writing this. I was literally sitting there, alone, making a joke about me drinking in the morning. I would often pull it together and stop drinking a few hours before my husband came home, so I could hide it. Or, I would try my very best to make him think the glass of wine in my hand when he got home at 5 pm was my first.

You see, one of the most prevalent things in most addiction stories is the secrecy and lying. I had become an expert at both. I knew that if anyone realized how much I was drinking, I would have to stop. And quite frankly, I wasn't ready to stop.

Within two years of my separating from the military, I was really a full-blown, semi-functioning alcoholic. I say semi-functioning because I was still somehow managing to operate my online boutique somewhat. Still, it wasn't thriving at all because alcohol was interfering! It's hard to get up and go to appointments to pick up clothes all over town when you are hungover!

Eventually, after trying and trying to do something with the boutique business, I had to let it go. I had gotten myself into debt trying a new "model" of purchasing bulk inventory and selling it instead of the consignment (business advice: don't ever keep tons of inventory on hand! It's THE worst thing an e-commerce business can do). I was sad to close the boutique, but it was a burden lifted. Plus…I had another idea brewing that felt like my BIG idea. It was one of those ideas that you think about and just get chills from.

New Business, Same Habits

As I was operating the online boutique, I became quite skilled in graphic design and website design. I was doing everything on my own and really just fell in love with design. I would stay up for literally hours into the morning to beautify the boutique website and create flyers and revamp the logo. I was doing these things more than actually selling the clothes! I had the most beautiful website but no customers. This was before I knew about the importance of messaging and client attraction! If there is no strategy behind what you are doing, your website and branding can be beautiful but still never attract bookers and buyers.

Anyway, as I was having all of this fun building the website and doing graphics, the thought came to my mind that I could actually do that for a living! I kept that thought quiet until I decided to close the online boutique business. The day after I closed it, I started researching how to open a graphic and website design business. These types of searches brought up people making $50 flyers and logos and $250 websites. So, I decided to charge $75 for websites, $25 for logos and go from there. I mean, I was inexperienced, so I wanted to get some work under my belt!

Business TIP: I am a firm believer that you cannot start charging like crazy when you are starting in a field that is NEW to you! When something is NEW to you, I believe you should start your pricing lower to learn your process, up-level your skills, and quite frankly, practice. This does not apply to those already an expert and just transitioning into having their own business or adding services to their expertise. In that case, you would need to lead with your correct and full pricing!

It would be almost 6 more years before I would be confident enough to raise my prices. You know why it took so long? Because it took me that long to stop trying to do everything alone!

So, I started charging next to nothing, with no real process or game plan as to how I was actually going to work with clients. I just knew I was going to make them some pretty websites for cheap. Besides friends and family, I really didn't know anyone who needed websites, so I started doing my first version of Instagram Marketing.

After about 6 months or so in business, and only getting a few referrals from friends and family, and one client that came across my website on Google because she Googled "cheap websites", I decided I wanted to start pitching to the clients I wanted directly via IG DM's. This was not a common tactic back then, so people were VERY open to having a conversation over DM or even passing me their number for a call. Listen, I was selling in the DM before all of these gurus came along doing it. However, because my pricing was awful and I had no strategy whatsoever, I wasn't able to actually leverage my methods. I gained clients who stayed with me for years that way.

However, they were not the people I needed to be around! They were people that were only there because I was "cheap". They would sing my praises all day, but bottom line, they stuck around because they liked being able to get a website or logo, or flyers, etc. for a fraction of the cost.

Let me paint you a picture so you can get a sense of who I was dealing with. THIS year, 2021, I've had 3 of the clients I was serving in the early years come back around (after disappearing for years) and ask me if I was available to help them with their websites. One of them wanted a full rebrand, and the others wanted "tweaks" (aka rebrands). When I told them my pricing, here was their responses:

1. I am not a millionaire yet, sorry, but no
2. Oh no, baby, we are in Covid…you can't charge those kinds of prices.
3. I thought it was too much when you were trying to charge me $400 before, absolutely not. This last lady was SO upset that I dared to even speak those new prices to her lol!

So, you can see the mindset of the people I was working with at this time. And you know what, it wasn't their fault that I wasn't raising my prices, it was mine! I thought so little of myself that any money was good enough. I had gotten so down in the dumps while I had the boutique, so used to people not even wanting to buy a $10 shirt from me that if someone wanted to pay me any amount of money, I was ok with it. Because in my mind, that meant I was operating a real business. Wow, if I only knew then what I knew now! But we learn lessons in the order we are supposed to, and I actually don't know if I would've been ready to receive it at that time.

My father's child

I was full throttle into my drinking by this point. I lost my father the day after my birthday in 2014, and the pain sent me down a path of destruction that I spent years on. There was no somewhat hiding it…I was drinking to the point of blacking out 3-4 days per week, and the other days I was barely functioning because of a raging hangover. There were days I would wake up shaking, and I knew what my body wanted. On those days, I would wait a little longer to start drinking or try to go without because it scared me that my body reacted that way.

The worst part of these days was the flashes of the night before that literally haunted me all day. Most of the time, I was a happy drunk, but sometimes I would have random memories pop into my head of being mean to my husband, literally yelling at him for not wanting to drink with me. It was bad ya'll. I also have memories of being on the phone with someone (I was that person who would call everyone and their momma when I got drunk…literally), and talking about God knows what. There are two phone conversations, in particular, I remember having that still break my heart today.

I'm not going to describe them to protect both my mom and my sister. Also, I refuse to give any power to things that were said and healed from.

I will, however, tell you what led to me finally realizing this pattern of drinking had to stop. Now mind you, I had tried to stop several other times before. In fact, a few times, I stopped because I was trying to "get healthy" and go on a diet. Every time I would start drinking again, I would tell myself I would keep it down to maybe a glass or two of wine. This ALWAYS escalates, period. It never stays just one or two glasses for more than a few weeks. Once that taste was back in my mouth, it was over. It may not be that very night that I have the wine, but it's like a poison, and literally, every time I stopped, when I started back up, it would come back with a vengeance.

The time before I quit for good, I started drinking again, and it was the worse it's ever been. The weeks before I quit again and had my final breakthrough, I threw up blood clots in my toilet several times and kept drinking. You guys, I was literally killing myself. I was keeping myself depressed and unhappy with this poison I was putting into myself. I was popping antacid pills just like my daddy. I was him. I was also smoking cigarettes like a chimney. You see how we go full circle? I was still that girl that cut her arm in JJ's bathroom.

Only now, I was throwing up blood instead of it having it gushing from my arm. It's impossible to cover up a gaping wound without treating it first. If you do, it will still get infected and eventually cause WAY more problems than the original injury. You might even lose a limb from infection! This is exactly what I was going through! My soul was infected, and it was seeping through anyway it could. I knew in the back of my mind that I need to make a change. It was heavy on my mind, and I started to feel more and more guilty about my drinking and what I knew I was doing to my body. I was also starting to have pains in my body that indicated that if I didn't change fast, I would be joining my father in an early grave. And that's just real. And then, Covid-19 happened.

Lesson 10

FINDING FAITH

When the news of Covid-19 started to reach the states, my husband and I had just gotten back from a mountain vacation with his brother and his girlfriend. As the country went further into lockdown, I went further down the bottle. You see, now, on top of being a full-fledged alcoholic, I also had anxiety to the point of shaking as I watched the daily Covid news. My journey to finding God again and getting sober is actually one that some may find funny. Heck, it sort of is now, but here goes.

Ya'll I thought I had The Rona! It was April 1st, 2020, and I had been up until about 3 am drinking. When I woke up this day, I just felt HOT! Like, it didn't feel like a normal hangover. I felt like my skin was literally burning off from the inside out. Part of me thought I had just finally done my liver in, the other part thought it was a normal hangover, but the largest part of me could have sworn it was Covid-19.

Because I felt so horrible, I continued to not drink

for days, and I continued to feel horrible for days. I was checking my temperature and had NO fever, but I was hot, I felt like I was having trouble breathing, but my oxygen levels were ok. I really think my body had just had enough of my shenanigans! My body was like sis; we need a break! So it literally refused to allow me to drink. This went on for about a week or so. Every day I would wake up, hoping I would be feeling back to normal, and every day I would wake up feeling the same horrible mess. Now, I just know someone is going to be like, GIRL you had Covid! Well, who knows, and honestly, it's not even relevant. Because what I'm going to tell you next is why I'm sitting here writing this book right now.

Breakthrough: Welcome Back

On April 4th, 2020, I gave my life back to God. I gave it to him fully, with every bone in my body. After this day, I was NOT the same, and I never will be again. My tears are streaming right now, and I will probably cry tears of absolute adoration and joy throughout the remainder of this short chapter. When you are reading this chapter, I want you to think back to when you met God. Like, really, really met God.

On the night of April 4th, I was feeling particularly bad. My skin felt like it was burning off, and I was in full-blown anxiety attack mode. I had tried taking a cold bath to no avail. So, after feeling like I was losing my mind and my husband thinking so as well, the only thing I knew to do was call my momma. When momma answered, I told her what had been going on. She asked me all of the "Covid questions," and I assured her I had no fever and I was breathing ok. So, she said she wanted to pray with me. As she prayed, I laid down in my bed facing up and closed my eyes. She went in! She prayed over me, prayed in tongues, and literally as I was lying there, I felt tingles all over my body. When she finished, she asked me in the most non-judgmental and loving way if I would please watch the sermon her pastor had posted online. Up until this point, I hadn't been to church in almost 20 years, and hadn't watched church online ever. If I did see something online, it was by accident, and I never sat down and actually watched it.

So, I told her I would watch the sermon. And after that amazing prayer she had just done, there was no way I was going to lie, lol! I tuned into her Pastors channel and saw that the name of the sermon was, "In A Crisis Turn To Him". This shocked me. Because I was definitely in crisis mode. At this point, not only was I sick physically, but I was also 4 days off of alcohol and having cravings.

I watched that sermon and felt a shift. It was like I could literally feel the air change direction. When the sermon was over, the pastor inviting everyone watching to give their life back to God. She said, if you are out there and you know it's time to come back home, lift your hands up with me and say this prayer. Right there in my living room chair, I lifted my hands to the ceiling and said that prayer with her. This was the first time I remember saying this prayer and actually feeling different. I mean, it felt like something was taking me over. The next thing I know, tears were streaming down my face and I was speaking in tongues.

I felt the urge to write, so I ran upstairs and grabbed my notebook. Notice I said "ran" upstairs? You see, when I say I felt brand new, I mean brand new physically as well. I am telling you God laid his hands on me that night. I started to feel cooler, and my headache went away, I just felt free. And I was about to get even freer as the Lord released an entire word to me!

Before I knew it, my notebook was a third of the way full, and I had written on every line. I had pulled up a gospel station on Spotify and was in worship and writing for close to 3 hours or more. It was just a surreal experience. I literally feel like I had an out-of-body experience that night. Around 3 am, I started to wind down, and the last song that started playing was "Come out of hiding". This was a call to action for me. I knew God was saying, "I gifted you with this breakthrough, now go tell the world. Tell them, so they will KNOW it was me when they see the elevation that is about to take place in your life".

That was my first act of outward obedience to him after giving my life back to God. I logged into Facebook and made a very long post about what I had experienced and how my life would now look different. To some, this may not seem like a big deal, but my Facebook was filled with people that knew I was a raging alcoholic because I had been out at the bars with them or calling them wasted. People that had seen or heard me talk about worshipping the universe instead of a God. People that had literally watched me up on the pole stripping. These people were the hardest and most judgmental group of people to tell! But God wanted me to get that out of the way. He needed me to make that move so he could go ahead and release blessings, and THAT HE DID!

Lesson 11

GETTING DOWN TO BUSINESS

Many times we don't realize how much of a blocker we are to our blessings. We will be standing smack dab in the way of things God is ready to release. Bigger things than we could ever hope for or imagine, and we will miss it because we are in our own way!

For the first 6 years of my business, I was in my own way. I turned my back on God and allowed addiction to overshadow everything God had planned for me. I chose to stay stuck. One of my coaches is always saying that "staying stuck is a choice". Well, I was definitely choosing stuck. I pretended to try, but I knew my habits and lack of faith were a problem. I was cancelling appointments regularly because I was hungover, then telling myself the client was just annoying because they wanted to get on the phone for no reason. Literally, I was passing blame to everyone else except me. The fact that I was able to keep this charade going for so long is a miracle to me.

However, when I stopped making excuses, gave my life back to God, and stopped drinking, my life changed. I described in the previous chapter how my life changed on a spiritual level, but it didn't stop there.

I went from earning no more than $3k per month in my business (a normal month was more like $500 during some seasons) to bringing in multiple six-figures this year! God has a HUGE plan for my life and the flood gates opened as soon as I submitted to him and let go of the things blocking me.

This chapter is where the meat is. I want you to get your pencil and notepad out because I am about to, for the first time to the public, break down HOW in the world this huge shift in my life came about.

The Confident Brand System

There was a very specific order in which things started to shift for my business. I say this because as I go through the steps I'm about to give you, many of you will be tempted to read ahead. I urge you not to do that. This entire book, I've been saying I want you to experience the breakthrough as you read. Well, this is the moment I have been preparing you for.

Step 1. Remove addictions. Now, I know that many of you

will say, "I'm not addicted to anything". Before you say that, think deeper. Addictions can run deep, and it doesn't have to be an addiction to drugs or alcohol! It can be food. Maybe you are over-indulging in sweets or caffeine? You can be addicted to drama in your life, so you always look for it and welcome it. You could be addicted to grief from losing a loved one that you refuse to let go of. You could be addicted to failure and the pity you get when you fail (sorry, just being real). You could be addicted to your job or your business, so you are overworking and neglecting your family. You could be addicted to being the "hero" of your family. You could be addicted to love or heartbreak. The list goes on. The definition of addiction is: *exhibiting a compulsive, chronic, physiological or psychological need for something.* If this at all sounds familiar about anything or anyone in your life. You need to address it and release it!

My drinking was a DIRECT barrier to my next level for over half a decade. I made excuses and choices that kept me from opening up the door to blessings. Don't let this be you. Make the changes you KNOW you have needed to make. Write a promise to yourself right now in your private notebook that you will address any addictions in your life. This first step is a must if you want to move to the next level.

Step 2. Solidify your faith. Yes, I put this after addiction. Because I truly believe that we need to take a step to show God, we are ready. So, once you have laid down addictions, get close to God and STAY close to God. This piece is something I was missing for 20yrs of my life. I kept trying to remove addiction and do better in business, but I was skipping this step.

Divine alignment is what put me in the direct path of other Christian women entrepreneurs online. Women that were a kingdom, but also making a lot of money in their businesses. I started stumbling upon rooms that put me in direct contact with other Holy Spirit-led women and other women who could help me level up in my business. This would prove to be KEY in my business success. God has been guiding me through every single decision I make (that's why I'm known for moving quickly on things, and it pays off!). From the coaches, I've worked with that have given me next-level strategies to the women of faith clients I have gotten to work with that have become dear friends. God has been my CEO, period. The game is played on a whole 'nother level when God is at point guard!

Step 3. Get aligned with people that can help elevate you! Get a coach, period. Ya'll I used to think coaching was some sort of "fluff" service that people who were trying to take people's money offered. I just didn't understand how a person could simply talk to someone and help them change their business. This was an example of me being bullheaded and staying ignorant about things! Even though I knew people that were greatly benefiting from coaching, I still didn't listen.

In 2019, I met a woman who was a coach, and she was just as crooked as could be. I luckily didn't hire her for those services, but it fed my belief that coaching was some sort of scam.

Well, I tell no lies when I say the strategies I have been able to develop from coaching have completely changed my life. And now, the coaching I am giving has changed my client's lives! It's a ripple effect.

Step 4. Get in the room! This one ties in directly with #3, but it's something all on its own. Sometimes, coaching is not just about getting 1:1 mentorship. It's about the ACCESS they have and can afford you! I gained a five-figure client from a newsletter one of my coaches sent out! Because their audience is so high-level, they trust this coach, and they can afford it. I mentioned being in the right environment earlier in this book. This is the same thing. Get in the right rooms, around people that can help you achieve your next level. You cannot continue to be in the room with people at your current level, then wonder why they can't help you move up!

They may not even have a vision for the next level yet! You need to be around people who have been where you are and help you see and achieve your next level. You need people with the vision to lead you. When you play only with those at your level, you are risking being in a "blind leading the blind" type of situation. It's unreasonable to ask someone who hasn't even made $100k yet to help you make $1million. So get in the right rooms.

Step 5. Brand yourself. This one is near and dear to my heart, not only because it's my passion, but because this is possibly THE most important thing I did, besides give my life back to God, to help my business accelerate at such an astronomical rate! When I learned the power of my message, I could leverage that to attract clients that I never thought I could obtain. In July of 2020, I had 700 followers on Instagram. About a month or so before, I had revisited my messaging to position myself in front of the women I wanted to serve. During that time, I crafted the messaging that has taken me from charging $1500 for full visual branding and web design in 2019 and part of 2020, to easily booking clients that will pay $20k.

Everyone's message is unique, and you must be under the helm of someone experienced when you are developing yours! While I do recommend you get a brand coach, I want to give you an extra nugget to take away because branding is such a passion of mine!

A. Uncover your overall objectives. What is your why? When you answer that, ask yourself why again until you have at least one sheet of paper filled. Keep going until you something stops you dead in your tracks. That's your why.

B. Assess Your Mindset. Where are you now, and where do

you need to be mindset-wise to go to your next level?
C. Assess who you want to serve (ideal client). Why? What can you help them with?
D. Nail down your messaging. How will you speak to this client? Why will they listen?
E. Create or develop your offers or products FOR your ideal clients. It's not about you; it's about them. Why do THEY want to read your book or sign up for your coaching program? Develop exactly what they need to achieve a transformation, not just what you feel like offering!
F. Lifestyle and Value price your offer. We don't price based on an hourly rate or what others are doing! You need to price based on the value you bring to the table in terms of expertise, experience, and education. Then also consider how much you need to make per year to live the life you want to! You cannot be hoping for 1million and only charging enough to make $50k…it doesn't add up. Charge correctly.
G. Get your visuals in order. Ya'll DO NOT skip this step. You will have done everything else in vain if you fail to attract clients to your online platform! Do not let your gifts fall on deaf ears because you didn't recognize the importance of visual branding. You need professional branded photos, a color palette, logo suite, and website for your visual branding.
H. Be consistent in all you do. This final piece of brand strategy is just overall advice. Do not set unrealistic goals,

instead set goals you know you can achieve and stay consistent with them.

6. Build Your Team. My recommendation is to start small but hire with purpose. Meaning, do not just run out and get a VA as your first hire because that's what everyone is doing. That may not strategically be the best first hire for you. When you are strategizing your brand and going through your processes, think about what sort of team member could do each process that you currently do in your business. Map out every single part.

7. Get your finances in order immediately! Separate your business finances from personal (Yes, even if you are a sole proprietor). You NEED to prepare for RAPID acceleration, so you need to be ready and set up legally. This is one area I wish I would have stewarded better. Because I literally jumped from making $3k in June to making $16k in July! It was that quick, and I was not ready in terms of my accounts and business paperwork.

8. Get your body ready. This final step may confuse some people, but it is just as important as the rest! Last year, right before God opened up the flood gates, he laid it on my heart to really start taking care of my body. He knew I was about to accelerate and would need to be mentally and physically prepared. Listen, I don't know what you have heard, but you

DO have to be ready to work.

You cannot be out here out of shape and tired trying to elevate to your next level. Now, that's some hard love for some of you, but it's true. Start taking care of the vessel God has given you so you can actually enjoy your next level. Steward every part of your life, including the temple God has blessed you with.

The blessing continues

God has given me a powerful testimony that I know will reach the people it is supposed to reach. Each and every one of you reading this book has been brought here for a reason. There are no accidents. There is something or several things in this book that you were supposed to read and take action on. You see, this book is not just another thing for you to consume, then put up on your shelf to gather dust. There is power in taking action at the moment! You've heard the testimony, and you have the steps, you know what's possible. Now, go forth and do! My story continues as does yours. Stay tuned for another great read as the journey and the lessons continue. God bless you!

ABOUT THE AUTHOR

Helping others turn dreams into reality is a labor of love for Krystal K. Portorreal, professional brand coach, author, designer and entrepreneur. As CEO of ADER Branding Company, she works with multi-talented women to create impactful brands that captivate audiences and generate next-level income. A highly relatable "brand guru" who inspires with knowledge, experience and humor, Krystal has worked with hundreds of clients since launching her company in 2014. Her passion for sharing the finer points of marketing and design comes matched only by her desire to see other women go after what they desire most out of life.

After serving in the Air Force for 10 years, Krystal became an entrepreneur and went back to school to study graphic design while building her business. She discovered she had a knack for helping women with beautiful design and finding the confidence required for a powerful brand. That is how her Confident Brand System was birthed.

When Krystal is not helping women build powerful brands, she enjoys a peaceful, quiet cabin, getaway with her husband Lavob, and pup Charlie.